MW00781930

MAKERS
of the
MUSLIM
WORLD

'Abd al-Rahman
b. 'Amr al-Awza'i

TITLES IN THE MAKERS OF THE MUSLIM WORLD SERIES

Series Editors: Professor Khaled El-Rouayheb, Harvard University,
and Professor Sabine Schmidtke, Institute for Advanced Study, Princeton

For current information and details of other books in the series, please visit
oneworld-publications.com/makers-of-the-muslim-world

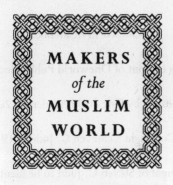

MAKERS
of the
MUSLIM
WORLD

'Abd al-Rahman
b. 'Amr al-Awza'i

STEVEN C. JUDD

ONEWORLD
ACADEMIC

Oneworld Academic

An imprint of Oneworld Publications

Published by Oneworld Academic, 2019

ISBN 978-1-78607-685-4
eISBN 978-1-78607-686-1

Typeset by Geethik Technologies
Printed and bound in Great Britain by Clays Ltd, Elcograf S.p.A.

Oneworld Publications
10 Bloomsbury Street
London WC1B 3SR
England

Stay up to date with the latest books,
special offers, and exclusive content from
Oneworld with our newsletter

Sign up on our website
oneworld-publications.com

To the memory of Michael Bonner, my teacher, mentor, and friend

CONTENTS

FOREWORD

This book is the product of a decades-long interest in al-Awza'i as both a religious scholar and a historical figure. It is in some ways a synthesis of a number of narrower projects that either focused on al-Awza'i, or in which he played an ancillary role. At the same time, this biography of al-Awza'i is part of a broader effort to revisit paradigms for understanding the Umayyad period and to create a more nuanced understanding of the emergence of Islamic law and theology.

In the text, I have minimized the use of Arabic terms, technical vocabulary, and diacritical marks. Dates appear with the hijri date followed by the common era date. Some readers will recognize the influences of earlier scholarship on my approach and will likely find allusions to my own previous arguments, as well as to approaches I have rejected. I have attempted, and likely at times failed, to note these influences where appropriate. Of course, any errors, omissions, or misinterpretations are mine alone.

The roster of colleagues who have contributed to this project, either directly or indirectly, has grown quite lengthy over its duration. Those who have shaped my thinking, offered new insights, and saved me from embarrassing pitfalls are too numerous to list here. However, I do want to offer special thanks to my colleagues in the History Department at SCSU who have read and commented on significant portions of this work, as well as my earlier pieces on al-Awza'i. They have been steadfast in their support and encouragement. I also thank SCSU for occasional course release time and a number of small grants that facilitated this project. I also thank Sabine Schmidtke and Jonathan Bentley-Smith at Oneworld for deeming al-Awza'i worthy of inclusion in the Makers of the Muslim World series and for their encouragement along the way. I also thank Michael Cook for his helpful suggestions for improving the work. Finally, and most importantly, I thank my family for their support and for tolerating both my occasional absences and more frequent absentmindedness.

It is my intention that this humble work on al-Awza'i will not be the last word on the subject. Instead, I hope that this book will inspire greater interest in this important contributor to early Islam. Given that so few words have been dedicated to understanding al-Awza'i and his impact, there are many more words to be written about him.

INTRODUCTION

'Abd al-Rahman b. 'Amr al-Awza'i is not widely remembered outside scholarly circles. Even among devout Muslims, he is not a household name, in contrast to some of his contemporaries. Most have at least a passing familiarity with Abu Hanifa, Malik b. Anas, al-Hasan al-Basri, and perhaps a few others from the second/eighth century. Al-Awza'i is, however, often overlooked, perhaps simply overshadowed by his more famous peers, despite his importance in the development of early Islam.

There are many explanations for al-Awza'i's relative obscurity. Unlike some of his contemporaries, al-Awza'i did not inspire a sizeable, determined cadre of followers to preserve his legacy and expand his influence. There are a variety of reasons for this, some of which will be explored in more detail. In addition, to an extent, al-Awza'i is the victim of the accidents of historical preservation. Later sources note several of his books and mention his correspondence with other scholars and government officials as well. However, his books have not survived, nor have many of his letters. Fragments survive here and there, but the corpus of extant writings ascribed to al-Awza'i is meager. Moreover, they appear to have disappeared from circulation not too long after his death. This is in part coincidental, but may also reflect the fact that he had few devoted followers to preserve his thoughts or ascribe additional words and ideas to him posthumously.

The tumultuous political climate surrounding the Abbasid revolution in 132/750 and the consequent marginalization of his Syrian homeland also contributed to al-Awza'i's obscurity. Unlike those contemporaries who ultimately became more famous, al-Awza'i was closely associated with the ousted Umayyad dynasty. Consequently, both his access to power and his circle of followers were disrupted. Revolutions do not necessarily doom scholars associated with the old regime to irrelevancy. Indeed, in many revolutions, including the Abbasid revolution, some members of the scholarly and bureaucratic elite retained or soon regained their stature under the new regime, which ultimately needed their talents. However, scholars like al-Awza'i, whose connections to the losing side were extensive, seldom reached their previous level of influence. Their dilemma was simple, but unavoidable. Clinging to their convictions about the virtues of the previous regime would have been an obviously faulty strategy for endearing themselves to the new regime. At the same time, however, malleably adapting and accepting the legitimacy of the revolution could have led to accusations of opportunism and sycophancy. Al-Awza'i's pre-revolutionary success and post-revolutionary legacy are topics that will be explored later in this work.

While al-Awza'i's immediate influence was short-lived, he did have a substantial impact on the formation of Islamic law and theology. To understand the process by which Islam matured and its doctrines were contested and articulated, it is important to broaden inquiry beyond those scholars who remain household names today. The early Islamic scholarly community was larger and more diverse in its viewpoints, and the refinement of the faith was not the exclusive domain of those who have been continually lauded in later times. Discrete studies of less renowned scholars can aid in understanding how the religion evolved and offer a more nuanced picture of early Islamic society generally.

Al-Awza'i is especially deserving of closer examination because of his unique position in the history of Islamic thought. His generation of scholars occupied a pivotal point in the development of Islamic law and theology. As mentioned above, they bridged the Umayyad and Abbasid eras and consequently had to navigate the complexities of a revolution infused with religious themes. They also lived in a time when the exemplars of the early days of Islam were no longer available as sources of guidance. The Prophet's companions were long since deceased, as were many of their immediate successors. The preservation of these luminaries' wisdom was now the responsibility of scholars more removed from the Prophet, both temporally and geographically. Al-Awza'i's generation also lived in a period when formal structures of religious authority did not yet exist, with the exception of the office of *qadi*, or religious judge, whose function, influence, and reputation were contested. Al-Awza'i's generation of scholars and their students began the process of creating legal and other structures for the preservation and dissemination of religious knowledge. It is important to note that al-Awza'i's contemporaries Abu Hanifa (d. 150/767) and Malik b. Anas (d. 179/796) became the earliest eponyms of legal *madhhab*s, or "schools" of legal thought. Al-Awza'i and his peers were formalizing legal and religious scholarship during a time of tremendous political disruption and revolution. The breakdown and reconstitution of centers of authority, religious and otherwise, complicated the lives of religious scholars in significant ways. Al-Awza'i and his peers were a point of stability in otherwise unstable times. Their interactions with political actors and each other were undoubtedly not always harmonious, but they represented a certain continuity in troubled times.

Al-Awza'i was particularly important in this context. Unlike his contemporaries, he was intimately associated with the Umayyad regime, where he influenced and was perhaps influenced by caliphal authority. Unlike many Umayyad loyalists, he not only survived the revolution, but continued to have an impact on legal and other matters despite his Umayyad past. In this regard he was unique among the generation of scholars who bridged the two eras. Consequently, al-Awza'i merits special consideration.

Al-Awza'i also stands out because he continued to be cited as an authority on Islamic legal and ritual questions even though his *madhhab* was short-lived. This in itself is somewhat remarkable. His followers had largely dissipated within one or two generations of his death, most affiliating with other legal *madhhab*s. They left no comprehensive written record of his views and accomplishments, no commentaries on his positions, and no evidence of an organized effort to perpetuate his tradition. Despite this, centuries later, scholars continued to cite al-Awza'i as an authority. These citations do not treat al-Awza'i as a representative of a lapsed school of thought, or as an example of parochial Syrian practice, or use him as a straw man to demonstrate doctrinal error. Instead, they typically treat him with the same respect that they show to his contemporaries whose *madhhab*s survived. Scholars who cited him adhered to a variety of later legal traditions and do not appear to have been trying simply to co-opt him into their school of thought. Al-Awza'i continues to be invoked by modern Islamic authorities as well, and even appears on occasion in modern debates surrounding ISIS and other controversial topics. His continued presence in the legal and ritual literature demonstrates that his personal authority survived despite his lack of an enduring institutional following. In this he is not unique. Others from his era, such as his colleague Sufyan al-Thawri (d. 161/778), continued to command respect as religious authorities without the benefit of long-lasting madhhabs to promote their brilliance. However, none of these other early Islamic scholars shares al-Awza'i's unique status during the Umayyad and early Abbasid periods. This combination of ongoing influence and unique experience makes al-Awza'i a relatively unknown figure who deserves additional attention.

In the chapters that follow, various aspects of al-Awza'i's influence will be examined in more detail. Chapter 1 offers a comprehensive discussion of the sources available for understanding al-Awza'i. It also addresses the difficulties encountered in examining a scholar whose corpus of work is lost (assuming it even existed), and explains how a tentative reconstruction of al-Awza'i's views remains possible despite these obstacles. Chapter 2 focuses on al-Awza'i's jurisprudence, for which he is most remembered. It offers a rudimentary reconstruction of his approach to law while acknowledging the limitations imposed by both the nature of the sources and the stage of Islamic legal development during his era. Chapter 3 describes the scholarly milieu in which al-Awza'i lived and worked. This chapter explains how a system of religious education functioned in an environment that lacked scholarly institutions. It focuses primarily on al-Awza'i's interactions with his contemporary peers and rivals, but also addresses practical matters such as financial concerns. Chapter 4 details al-Awza'i's views on theological questions and the extent of his influence in early theological debates. It underscores connections between theological and legal reasoning as well. While most discussions of early Islamic scholars focus on legal issues, this chapter will emphasize that theological issues were equally important and in many ways more contentious. Chapter 5 discusses al-Awza'i's complicated political entanglements and encounters with both the Umayyad and Abbasid regimes. It describes his role at the Umayyad caliphal court and explains how he managed to survive the dynasty's demise and earn the respect of the Abbasids despite his loyalty to their foes. Finally, chapter 6 charts al-Awzaʻi's enduring legacy, describing how he was remembered in the centuries after his death, how modern scholars have interpreted him, and the manner in which he is still invoked by modern Muslim legal scholars.

Before turning to these topical discussions, however, a short biographical sketch is in order. This basic description of al-Awzaʻi's life will not be painstaking in its detail, but will illustrate some of the frustrations inherent to reconstructing the biography of an important but poorly documented second/eighth-century scholar.

AL-AWZA'I'S BIOGRAPHY

Details of al-Awza'i's early life are scant and are the subject of some disagreement. Sources even diverge about his exact name and its meaning. He is typically identified as 'Abd al-Rahman b. 'Amr Abu 'Amr al-Awza'i. One source claims that his given name was 'Abd al-'Aziz and that he later changed it to 'Abd al-Rahman. No reason is given for his purported decision to change his name. He is most often addressed simply as al-Awza'i, an unusual name whose origins are more contested. Some reports suggest that the label derives from a minor sub-clan of the Himyar (or perhaps Hamadan) tribe in Yemen. At least one authority suggested the name originated from Sind, in non-Arab eastern Iran, despite the fact that al-Awza'i firmly asserted that he was of Arab genealogy and was born in the Beqaa Valley, near Baalbek. Many reports indicate that the name derives from the neighborhood where he lived, just outside the walls of Damascus, though geographical sources do not label the neighborhood as al-Awza'. There is even speculation that the neighborhood was labeled al-Awza' because members of this obscure sub-tribe lived there. At least three other Damascene scholars, all of minor importance, were referred to as al-Awza'i. Their brief biographical notices suggest that the name referred to the neighborhood rather than to a tribal splinter. Of course, this does not preclude the possibility that the neighborhood was named for the tribesmen who settled there. Regardless of its origins, the name al-Awza'i remained unusual. If it derived from tribal roots, few if any persevered in embracing the label. If al-Awza' was a neighborhood, almost no other residents claimed it as their moniker and it quickly fell out of use as a place name as well. His distinctive name is one of the many puzzles about al-Awza'i's early life.

There is broad agreement that al-Awza'i was born in 88/707, although the exact location of his birth and the circumstances of his childhood are less certain. He is generally reported to have been born in a small village somewhere in the vicinity of Baalbek, though no specific town is mentioned in the sources. His father, 'Amr b. Yuhmad was an unknown figure who died while al-Awza'i was quite young. It does not appear that 'Amr was a scholar or came from a prominent family. Some suggest that he was quite elderly, possibly in his seventies, when al-Awza'i was born. There are no reports regarding any siblings al-Awza'i may have had either. After 'Amr's death, his widow and son lived an itinerant life around Baalbek for an undefined period of time before settling in Damascus. Here al-Awza'i began studying *hadith* (sayings of the Prophet) under the guidance of an unnamed teacher who may have been his uncle, whose support may also have been the impetus for his mother to settle in Damascus in the first place.

When al-Awza'i was older, likely in his late teens, he received an appointment in Yamama, in eastern Arabia. Sources do not describe the nature of the office to which he was assigned or the process by which he received the post. Whatever the nature of his work there, it resulted in his enrollment in the *diwan* (pension registry), which provided him with income to suppport his scholarly endeavors. It also facilitated his work in Yamama with Yahya b. Abi Kathir (d. 129/747), who became one of his principal scholarly mentors. After a few years there, al-Awza'i embarked upon a further quest for knowledge, traveling to Basra in 110/728 with the intention of studying with al-Hasan al-Basri and Ibn Sirin. Unfortunately, al-Hasan died while al-Awza'i was en route and Ibn Sirin died shortly after his arrival, denying the young scholar the opportunity to learn from either of these revered figures. It is unclear where al-Awza'i's study tour took him after this setback. Lists of his teachers in biographical sources include few Basrans, suggesting that he moved on rather than making the best of things in Basra. Most of his teachers were from either Damascus or Medina. The sources do not indicate that he resided in Medina for any period of time, suggesting that his learning at the feet of Medinan scholars took place during his pilgrimage trips to the Hijaz instead. Compared to some of his contemporaries, his scholarly travel was limited. In particular, his forays eastward were unusually sparse and it is striking that he apparently did not detour to Kufa after his Basran disappointment. Perhaps he found his eastern colleagues lacking, or perhaps enough of them flowed through Damascus and Medina to have precluded any necessity for further travel.

Sometime before 113/731, al-Awza'i returned to Damascus, where he continued his studies and developed his reputation as a scholarly authority. His biographers typically note that he was first sought out for his legal expertise in 113/731, when he was twenty-five years old. They do not clarify who first asked him for advice or what query he answered; although it is widely reported that he ultimately responded to more than seventy thousand legal questions during his lifetime. This is likely an exaggeration, given that even the most prolific of scholars could scarcely address approximately five distinct legal questions per day for a period of over forty years. Unfortunately, as chapter 2 will demonstrate, very few of these thousands of answers to legal questions survive.

At some point after his return to Damascus, likely around the time he was recognized as a legal authority, al-Awza'i gained the attention of the caliph Hisham (r. 105/724–125/743), who relied on him for both legal and theological guidance. The exact nature of their relationship is amorphous and will be discussed in detail in chapter 5. While al-Awza'i had no formal title, he was a common presence at the caliphal court of Hisham for over a decade. After his employer/patron died in 125/743, al-Awza'i retired to Beirut, which is often portrayed as his hometown, despite the fact that he does not appear to have lived there until he was in his late thirties. From his base in Beirut, which was still considered to be on the frontier because of its importance as a starting point for various expeditions by land and sea, al-Awza'i continued to offer legal and other advice until his death in 157/774. There is some indication that he spent time farther north on the Byzantine frontier as well, though the dates and nature of his service there are not preserved. His close association with specific legal and strategic questions relating to the Byzantine frontier make clear that, regardless of his physical location, he was in regular consultation with those on the front lines.

Stories of al-Awza'i's death add a strange twist to his life of pious service. He was reportedly found in the bath at his home, where he expired after being accidentally locked in, either by his wife or a servant. Naturally, he was found facing Mecca, apparently meeting his end engaged in prayer, even while enjoying the luxury of the bath. Reports of his funeral and burial emphasize both the size of the crowd and its ecumenical nature, with Jews and Christians joining the procession and participating in prominent ways. The significance of these tales, which may be legendary, will be addressed in chapter 6. Al-Awza'i was reportedly survived by several sons. Only one of them, Muhammad b. 'Abd al-Rahman, appears to have attempted to follow his father's path into scholarly life, though with considerably less success. His wife's son from a previous marriage, Yahya b. 'Abdallah also earns mention as a minor scholar. The identities of his other children and extended family are unknown.

Given his prominence as a scholar and a courtier at the Umayyad caliphal court, it is disappointing that details of many aspects of al-Awza'i's life have not been preserved. His biography is not, however, unusual. The early lives of scholars and political leaders of his era are not generally well documented. It is surprising, for instance, that al-Awza'i's birthdate is agreed upon; in many instances such basic details are much-contested. The fact that, by all accounts, al-Awza'i did not come from an elite family makes the ambiguity about his early life typical. Such information was not recorded and was not seen to be important. Indeed, for students to query their busy teacher about his childhood rather than about his views on crucial legal and doctrinal questions would be considered odd and unproductive, perhaps even irritating. The lack of details about his later life may reflect, at least in part, the tumultuous circumstances of the time combined with the rapid dissolution of his scholarly following. The proliferation of biographical details, real or imagined, about the founders of legal schools demonstrates to an extent the proliferation of the schools themselves. Al-Awza'i's legacy did not benefit from such expansive hagiographical efforts.

In the chapters that follow, details about aspects of al-Awza'i's life and thoughts on crucial issues will be reconstructed from the record that remains scattered in a variety of later sources. In many cases, these reconstructions will be somewhat speculative, and caveats will abound. While this may at times frustrate the reader, tentative conclusions, vague explanations, and occasional lacunae must remain in order to be true to the sources, which will be discussed in more detail in the following chapter.

THE SOURCES

For historians of any period, finding adequate, reliable sources is a priority, and often a problem. In this regard, the early Islamic period is not exceptional, although the difficulties presented by early Islamic sources are particularly serious and raise doubts about how accurately the early Islamic past can be described. Before embarking on an attempt to reconstruct the life and thought of al-Awza'i and the milieu in which he lived and worked, it is important to consider the state of the sources and what they can and cannot reveal about the Umayyad and early Abbasid period and about al-Awza'i and other religious scholars of that era.

Studies of the history of any aspect of early Islam cannot rely on contemporaneous sources, because they are largely nonexistent. Archival material, a favorite for most historians, has not survived from the first/seventh- and second/eighth-century Middle East. For the earliest period, this is not surprising. The chaos of rapid expansion, along with an approach to government that was largely ad hoc, relying on loose tribal organization, was not conducive to record keeping in any comprehensive way.

By al-Awza'i's time, however, the Umayyads had developed more sophisticated, bureaucratic forms of government, drawing on the examples of the defeated but bureaucratically competent Byzantines and Sassanians. Surely they had come to accept the benefits (and perhaps annoyances) of record keeping. Later sources offer evidence that the Umayyads, and perhaps even the Rashidun before them, did indeed document their activities and finances. Some early histories mention caliphal scribes and occasionally even identify them by name.

The maintenance of official registers (*diwans*) attracts some attention in later sources, and individuals are sometimes noted to have been listed in the *diwan*, which entitled them to a pension. Later historical sources mention correspondence between caliphs and regional officials, sometimes even reproducing these early letters. At the very least, the authors of these later sources worked under the assumption that the Umayyads wrote letters, kept records, and employed bureaucrats to perform these functions.

Unfortunately, the products of these early scribes and accountants do not survive in their original form. If the Umayyads archived such records, those archival collections have not survived. Some early Islamic papyri have been found, including a fair number whose content is administrative in nature. While these discoveries confirm that Umayyad-era officials did keep written records, they remain too few and fragmentary to draw broad conclusions about Umayyad administration. In recent years, these documents have attracted increased attention. Additional discoveries, along with further study, compilation, and authentication of these artifacts may provide at least a fragmentary archive from the Umayyad period at some point in the future.

Unless and until such an archive of contemporary material is collected, scholars researching the early Islamic period must rely primarily on later narrative sources and grapple with the problems these retellings of history present. In this regard, early Islamic history is not unique. If contemporary, datable, authenticated archival material were a prerequisite for writing history, much of pre-modern and especially ancient history would be relegated to the realm of myth and legend. Scholars should be no more or less skeptical about narratives of the Islamic past than they are about stories of any society's past.

The principal sources used for reconstructing early Islamic history are chronicles which began to appear in the third/ninth century and multiplied shortly thereafter. These works were at times voluminous and presented sweeping narratives, often purporting to cover all of human history. The goals of the compilers of these works are hard to fathom, particularly since they were reticent about elaborating on the meaning of the stories they told. These grand works do, however, include citations of earlier works, many of which are otherwise lost.

As mentioned above, these citations include letters, sermons, and other lengthy quotations. One seldom finds clear evidence that the chroniclers relied on written sources, because citations are presented under the guise of oral transmission. Mentioning a book title from an earlier authority would ruin the illusion of orality, even though it was well known that some early scholars had many books. The accuracy of citations of earlier works is sometimes debated. There is evidence of paraphrasing, or perhaps alternative recensions of the earlier material. In some cases, the chronicles even demonstrate confusion about the basic chronology of events. Despite their shortcomings, these chronicles, especially al-Tabari's (d. 310/923) *Ta'rikh al-rusul wa'l-muluk* (History of Prophets and Kings), provide the scaffolding upon which most accounts of Islamic history are built.

Outside the narrative works dating from the fourth/tenth century, there are few additional sources for the early period. Non-Arabic sources are surprisingly few, given that the neighboring Byzantine Empire and now defunct Sassanian Empire were both literate and bureaucratic. A few non-Arabic sources describe the events of the early Islamic period, but at times confuse rather than enlighten. Their chronologies are sometimes out of sync with the Arabic tradition. Whether this represents confusion on the part of the non-Arab chroniclers or reflects efforts to tidy up the flow of events in the Arabic sources is difficult to ascertain. The non-Arabic sources also offer little information on the inner workings of the rising Islamic empire. Their authors were too separated from the new rulers' inner circles to be aware of their intricacies. The lack of a more extensive non-Arabic record of the period is a reminder that the paucity of sources is not a problem distinct to the Arabic tradition. Perhaps this merely underscores the collapse and fragmentation of Byzantine and Sassanian society in the face of the Arab expansion, or perhaps it illustrates a broader indifference to archiving and chronicling during the period.

In addition to written sources, archeological remains and numismatic evidence can be somewhat helpful for reconstructing events. However, these resources are also fragmented. For the current study, a biography of a particular scholar, these sources, even if they were abundant, cannot be very helpful. Coins may allow one to identify rulers and governors and to locate mints, but they do not tell stories of scholars and their views. Indeed, early Islamic coins do not even reveal who ran the mints in which they were cast. Later chronicles must be relied upon to fill such gaps. Archeological sources are similarly unhelpful for the current task. Scholars did not build anything distinctive, except the collection of books in their libraries. As discussed already, early scholars' books have not survived.

Given that the reconstruction of early Islamic history is dependent almost entirely on written narratives produced centuries after the events they describe, it is to be expected that there is widespread, at times contentious debate about the usefulness of these later sources. The historiographical discussion about these issues is substantial, reflecting a wide variety of methods of gauging the veracity of Arabic texts. Much of this debate is highly technical. Some recent works have introduced digital, big data tools to the discussion. Many of the works on the topic end up being highly polemical. Retracing the details of these disputes is beyond the scope of the current work.

In general, though, modern scholars' judgments of the Arabic sources and their reliability have run the full gamut of extremes. Some scholars accept nearly everything they read at face value, even when there are contradictions. Others show a strong preference for particular sources against which they judge the quality of all others. It is also troubling that researchers at times engage in cherry-picking, plucking only snippets that support their scholarly, religious, or political agendas. Given the controversial role early Islam plays in modern discourse, this is not surprising. Finally, at the far extreme, a few scholars have taken an extremely skeptical view of the sources, rejecting anything that cannot be corroborated by material outside the Arabic tradition as mere myth and legend.

This study will take a cautious, but not entirely skeptical approach to the sources. Obviously, scholars should not believe everything they read, but neither should they reject everything. It is important to recognize that even seemingly objective chroniclers had agendas to pursue and axes to grind. While their biases are not always instantly apparent, an effort should be made to uncover them. This is especially important when approaching topics like al-Awza'i, where biases and lacunae in the sources present serious challenges.

The first general obstacle to overcome is the fact that al-Awza'i was, for the most part, remembered as an Umayyad-era figure. The Umayyads present a special historiographical problem in that their story is viewed exclusively through the lens of scholars working during the Abbasid era. As discussed above, later sources do preserve some earlier material, at least in fragmentary form. However, the frenzy of collecting, collating, and writing historical narratives for the Umayyad period only began in the late third/ninth century, long after the dynasty's demise. At worst, these Abbasid-era sources can embody an attitude of Abbasid triumphalism and exhibit disdain for the defeated Umayyads. At best, they were written by scholars seeking to be objective, but with the knowledge that the Umayyad regime had failed. It was natural for these later scholars to focus on perceived origins of Umayyad decay, either to explain what went wrong or to caution or admonish their own rulers. Put simply, knowing how the Umayyad story ended affected how it was written.

In the case of al-Awza'i, there are more specific pitfalls. As will be discussed below, he was a respected legal scholar whose own writings are mostly lost. He was a mentor to numerous students who, with a few exceptions, apparently did not write about their teacher and his teachings. Perhaps most significantly, al-Awza'i had strong political and patronage ties to the Umayyad caliphs and a difficult relationship with the Abbasid authorities. The Abbasid revolution not only undermined his career, it dramatically affected how he was remembered.

Given his apparent lack of written output and his delicate political situation, it is significant, perhaps surprising, that any traces of his legal thought survive. The preservation of legal material and anecdotes about al-Awza'i illustrates that later historical and legal sources did not reject Umayyad-era figures automatically, even if they were associated with the defunct regime. This should offer some reassurance that later, Abbasid-era texts are not entirely blinded by ideological concerns. The survival of material about al-Awza'i in these texts also underscores his importance as a legal scholar. Despite the fact that he had few if any followers by the time works discussing him were composed, and despite his ties to the old regime, his views and deeds still merited preservation and were considered valuable.

There are indications that al-Awza'i did indeed write legal works and that these works remained in circulation for at least a time after his death. The *Fihrist* (catalogue) of the tenth-century Baghdad book-dealer Ibn al-Nadim (d. 380/990) includes two works by al-Awza'i. These have rather generic titles: *Kitab al-sunan fi'l-fiqh* (Book of the Sunna in Jurisprudence) and *Kitab masa'il fi'l-fiqh* (Book of Questions about Jurisprudence). Ibn al-Nadim credits other scholars with works with the exact same titles, suggesting perhaps that these are not actual titles but descriptions of the works' contents. Neither of these books is extant and neither is cited by name in any later legal works. It is still possible that they were utilized by later legal scholars describing al-Awza'i's views, since book titles are rarely mentioned in early Islamic legal writings. It is also possible that the snippets of quotations from al-Awza'i found in later works are derived from these two books without citation. However, the available sources make it impossible to prove this definitively. What is clear is that al-Awza'i's writings remained relevant enough to be part of a bookdealer's inventory two centuries after his death. Why they subsequently disappeared from circulation remains an unanswered, perhaps unanswerable, question.

A third work by al-Awza'i, his *Kitab al-siyar* (Book on the Laws of War), is better preserved. It does not appear on Ibn al-Nadim's list despite the fact that the *Kitab al-siyar* is the only one of al-Awza'i's works cited by name in later sources. This anomaly is difficult to explain. The work attracted the attention of al-Awza'i's rivals and their disciples and was also cited in scholarly works produced in Baghdad a few decades before Ibn al-Nadim's time. It seems unlikely that al-Awza'i's work somehow did not merit inclusion in the Baghdad bookdealer's inventory, that citations in later sources could have rendered the original superfluous, or that it was originally merely a chapter of one of the other works mentioned. Ibn al-Nadim does mention that al-Tabari's compilations included al-Awza'i's *Siyar*, but does not treat it as a separate work. Nor does Ibn al-Nadim appear to have been aware of the *Kitab al-siyar* of al-Awza'i's student, al-Fazari. Perhaps this is simply a reminder that, for all its merits, Ibn al-Nadim's list may not have been complete, but was merely a snapshot of the Baghdad market of his day.

Three later sources include extensive citations of al-Awzaʻi's *Siyar*. The earliest of these is Abu Yusuf's *Radd ʻala siyar al-Awza ʻi* (Refutation of al-Awzaʻi's *Siyar*). Abu Yusuf (d. 182/798) was a student of al-Awzaʻi's great rival Abu Hanifa (d. 150/767) and wrote his refutation in response to al-Awzaʻi's criticism of his master. The work contains significant quotations from al-Awzaʻi's works but also ascribes a few repulsive views to al-Awzaʻi that are not attested in other sources. Its usefulness as a repository of al-Awzaʻi's views is somewhat tainted by its polemical nature. Not long after Abu Yusuf's work, Muhammad b. Idris al-Shafiʻi (d. 205/820) included excerpts from al-Awzaʻi's *Siyar* in his massive work of jurisprudence, the *Kitab al-umm* (The Exemplar). Unlike Abu Yusuf, he does not appear to have been determined to rebut al-Awzaʻi's views explicitly, but rather to catalogue them and contrast them to the views of others. Finally, the great chronicler and Qurʼan commentator al-Tabari (d. 310/923) included references to al-Awzaʻi's *Siyar* in his *Ikhtilaf al-fuqaha'* (Disagreements among the Jurists). Here again, the intention appears to have been to catalogue divergent views on a variety of legal questions rather than to refute al-Awzaʻi.

The citations in these works are surprisingly consistent with each other, suggesting that they may have drawn from the actual lost work of al-Awzaʻi. However, even if they are accurate, it cannot be assumed that these excerpts represent the entirety of al-Awzaʻi's *Kitab al-siyar*. It is also significant that these excerpts were not produced by students of al-Awzaʻi or by later adherents to his views, but rather by representatives of rival legal traditions. On the one hand, their interest in his work underscores al-Awzaʻi's significance as a legal authority, even centuries after his death. On the other hand, the possibility that these sources may have distorted al-Awzaʻi's positions or omitted vital information cannot be ignored.

Further complicating matters is the fact that one of al-Awzaʻi's students, Abu Ishaq al-Fazari (d. 185/802) wrote extensively about al-Awzaʻi's views on warfare in his own *Kitab al-siyar*, but did not mention al-Awzaʻi's book specifically. While most of the positions he ascribed to al-Awzaʻi are consistent with those attested in the works discussed above, it is clear that al-Fazari was not copying or even paraphrasing the same work they used. Al-Fazari's work raises a number of questions. It seems peculiar that one of al-Awza'i's most dedicated students would not cite the only one of his master's works other scholars acknowledged by name. Did al-Fazari consider his own notes superior to his master's book? Did he somehow not have a copy of al-Awza'i's *Siyar*? How did Abu Yusuf in distant Baghdad have a book by al-Awza'i that al-Fazari apparently lacked? These questions, combined with Ibn al-Nadim's omission of al-Awza'i's *Kitab al-siyar* from his *Fihrist* raise doubts about how widely this work circulated and how important it really was.

Another curious repository of material from al-Awza'i can be found in the introductory volume (*Taqdima*) of Ibn Abi Hatim al-Razi's *Kitab al-jarh wa'l-ta'dil* (Book of Critique and Verification). Ibn Abi Hatim (d. 327/938) wrote his *Jarh* as an aid to evaluating *hadith* transmitters and the veracity of their reports. The *Taqdima* is sometimes treated as an introduction to this work, but is occasionally considered a separate work, given its different organizational scheme. Ibn Abi Hatim compiled a long series of reports about al-Awza'i in the *Taqdima*. Much of the material can be found in other biographical works discussed below. However, the unique feature of the *Taqdima* is that it includes a series of letters al-Awza'i purportedly wrote during his long retirement in Beirut. The letters are addressed to a variety of Abbasid officials, ranging from local functionaries to the caliph himself. They are essentially petitions for redress written on behalf of local residents who had been treated badly by Abbasid officials, or whose problems had been ignored. They include pleas for prisoners to be ransomed from their Byzantine captors, complaints about excessive tax burdens placed on local Christians, and other appeals for justice. Unfortunately, Ibn Abi Hatim does not indicate whether or not al-Awza'i's entreaties were successful.

Modern scholars, even those skeptical of the Arabic sources, have generally accepted the authenticity of these pieces of correspondence. This collection of letters is important for several reasons. Assuming the letters are authentic, this is essentially a reproduction of a fragmentary archive of al-Awza'i's correspondence. In a setting where such documentation is meager, that in itself is exciting. Unfortunately,

Ibn Abi Hatim's archive does not provide much context for the letters and it is hard to pinpoint most of the historical events to which they refer. Nor does he include responses from Abbasid officials. Despite this, the letters do offer glimpses of life on the Byzantine-Muslim frontier, and they give insights into the real problems local communities there faced. It is also significant that these were written after al-Awza'i's retirement to Beirut. The fact that local residents would seek out al-Awza'i to advocate on their behalf demonstrates that he still enjoyed a degree of influence with the Abbasids, despite his past association with the Umayyads. Few if any former Umayyad advisers could scold local officials, much less expect responses from the Abbasid caliph himself. Al-Awza'i clearly still commanded some importance. Indeed, the mere fact that Ibn Abi Hatim found his letters worth copying and preserving is a testament to al-Awza'i's stature.

Unfortunately, the search for material directly attributable to al-Awza'i yields rather paltry results. We are left with two lost books that no later scholar cited, a third book that is frequently cited by al-Awza'i's opponents but not by his own students and that was not independently extant two centuries after his death, and a series of letters written during his retirement. A biography of al-Awza'i written solely on the basis of his own writings would be a rather slim work.

Fortunately, shorter fragments of work attributable to al-Awza'i can be found in other sources. These traces present their own challenges, but can provide a few more details about al-Awza'i and his thought. Like most early Islamic scholars, al-Awza'i was recognized as a *muhaddith*, a transmitter of prophetic *hadith*. Reports transmitted by al-Awza'i are found in each of the major *hadith* collections compiled in the third/ninth and fourth/tenth centuries. These reports have limited utility for reconstructing al-Awza'i's approach to religious and legal questions. Like other *muhaddith*s, he appears in the collections as a transmitter of reports, not as a commentator. These reports can confirm the identities of some of al-Awza'i's teachers and students, though such material is also found in the biographical compendia discussed below. While al-Awza'i's thought process is not evident in these *hadith* reports, they do illustrate areas of law and ritual in which he was interested. An abundance of reports on some topics and an absence of any on other topics might provide clues about his legal focus. However, the usefulness of such data is inherently limited.

Additional legal and ritual material from al-Awza'i is preserved in a variety of later texts of the *ikhtilaf* genre. These works were dedicated to documenting disagreements between early Islamic scholars over particular aspects of law and ritual. The earliest such texts date from the early fourth/tenth century and the genre quickly developed a standard organization and form. A particular question is posed, followed by the answers of any number of legal scholars, sometimes simply listing who agreed or disagreed with whom. Some of these works merely catalogue opinions, while others focus on illustrating the correctness of a particular school's doctrine. Ultimately, these works grew to include myriad queries about sometimes narrow, even peculiar, legal distinctions.

Most of the *ikhtilaf* works cite al-Awza'i at least occasionally. While he does not appear as frequently as several other scholars, some works still include hundreds of citations of his opinions, providing a significant amount of material. These works contribute to a better understanding of al-Awza'i in several ways. It is striking that the views ascribed to him in different works are remarkably consistent; sometimes they appear almost verbatim. This suggests that the *ikhtilaf* compilers drew upon a fixed corpus of material regarding al-Awza'i's views, perhaps even the lost works in Ibn al-Nadim's catalogue. At the very least, there appears to have been widespread agreement about what al-Awza'i thought about particular issues, making it possible to use these sources to reconstruct at least a partial picture of his views. It is also important to note once again that al-Awza'i remained important enough to merit citation in these works centuries after his death.

There remain, however, significant limitations to the usefulness of the *ikhtilaf* literature. Like the *siyar* material, these works were not compiled by al-Awza'i's followers, but by scholars who either saw him as a representative of rival viewpoints, or as historical relic. The possibility of bias cannot be ignored. A second limitation is that the *ikhtilaf* works frustratingly do not cite their written sources. Any suggestion that their authors had al-Awza'i's lost books at their disposal must remain tentative, and the possibility that they utilized some

other, unknown compilation of his views remains. Finally, while the
ikhtilaf works provide traces of al-Awza'i's thoughts, they do not discuss his methods, but merely note his conclusions about particular
questions. In some cases, his legal methods may be implicitly obvious, but often they are not. Given the small amount of material these
citations include, it remains difficult to evaluate his legal approach on
their basis.

The Arabic biographical sources also contain significant material
on al-Awza'i. These works preserve biographical data on scholars and
political figures whom the works' compilers considered important
enough to include. The earliest such works focused on *muhaddith*s and
were written to assist scholars in their evaluation of *isnad*s (chains of
transmission) used to authenticate prophetic *hadith*. Later examples
broadened their scope to include political figures, assorted holy men,
poets, and others. Some focused on followers of particular legal *madhhab*s, while others focused on important people from specific cities or
regions. Their organizational schemes and criteria for inclusion varied,
but the individual biographies tended to have similar structures and
content.

Al-Awza'i appears in each of the standard biographical works on
hadith transmitters. His status as a respected *muhaddith* assured his
inclusion in such works. The data found in most of these is similar,
focusing on the identities of his students and teachers while adding a
few anecdotes about his transmission of *hadith*. Most of the entries are
brief, sometimes less than a single page, as is typical for works focusing on *muhaddith*s. Their purpose is simply to verify who transmitted
to and from whom and to evaluate the reliability of *muhaddith*s. The
compilers of these works did not intend to offer complete, narrative
biographies of their subjects.

More data on al-Awza'i can be found in works that include a broader
range of subjects. For instance, Abu Nu'aym al-Isfahani's *Hilyat
al-awliya'* (The Ornament of the Saints) includes more narrative anecdotes about al-Awza'i, with an emphasis on his piety. Abu Nu'aym's
(d. 430/1038) purpose differed from that of the *hadith* critics. He
focused on the spiritual side of Islam, collecting biographies of exemplary mystics, ascetics, and other pious individuals. Consequently,

he included details about al-Awza'i and others that the *hadith* critics
might have found superfluous to their purposes.

City histories of Damascus also include a great deal of material
about al-Awza'i. The compilers of city histories sought to provide
expansive, often laudatory descriptions of their cities. Toward that
end, they included stories about the great men who called these cities
their homes. The criteria used for inclusion were broad, allowing for
descriptions of political and military leaders, and even merchants, in
addition to religious scholars. Abu Zur'a al-Dimashqi (d. 281/894)
produced the earliest surviving city history of Damascus. His *Ta'rikh*
(History) includes a fair amount of material about al-Awza'i, though it
is spread throughout the work rather than compiled into a tidy biography. He includes discussions about al-Awza'i's merits as a *muhaddith*,
which largely parallel what is found in the compilations by the *hadith* critics. He also records a number of anecdotes about al-Awza'i's
interactions with political elites and others in the city, offering a more
nuanced image of al-Awza'i and the environment in which he lived
and worked.

The most extensive and impressive collection of material about
al-Awza'i is found in Ibn 'Asakir's *Ta'rikh madinat Dimashq* (History
of Damascus). Ibn 'Asakir (d. 571/1176) was a meticulous polymath
who wrote this massive work to document the glories of Damascus.
Its eighty volumes include biographies of more than ten thousand
important people who were natives and/or residents of Damascus,
or in some cases merely famous travelers who passed through. He
drew on a broad array of sources; some of them survive but many are
otherwise lost. His entry on al-Awza'i is eighty-two pages long, by
far the most complete extant biography of him. In addition, al-Awza'i
appears in a number of biographies of other Damascenes with whom
he interacted. While there are curious omissions from Ibn 'Asakir's
treatment of al-Awza'i, and it demonstrates occasional hints of hagiography, Ibn 'Asakir's *Ta'rikh* remains the most useful text for reconstructing al-Awza'i's life and work.

Despite being a relatively late source, Ibn 'Asakir provides an
important perspective on al-Awza'i. His focus on Damascus and its
exemplary residents helps to compensate for some of the biases in

other sources. Al-Awza'i's association with the Umayyads was less problematic for Ibn 'Asakir, since their reign represented a glorious period in the city's history. The fact that al-Awza'i's *madhhab* (legal school) did not survive is also less important, since its brief prominence provides evidence of Damascus' contribution to the development of Islamic law. While the Abbasid caliphs still commanded putative loyalty, Ibn 'Asakir's patron, Nur al-Din (d. 569/1174), was more concerned with Damascus than with distant Baghdad. The detailed attention Ibn 'Asakir devotes to al-Awza'i underscores his prominence in Syrian historical memory, even four centuries after his death. However, a degree of caution must remain, given the hagiographic undertones of the work.

Despite al-Awza'i's importance as a religious scholar and his connections to the Umayyad caliphs, the major chronicles barely mention him. While earlier material on al-Awza'i, such as that cited by Ibn 'Asakir, was likely available to al-Tabari and other chroniclers, they chose not to use it. Their purpose was different from that of the city historians and *hadith* critics. Military and political matters dominate the chronicles. Legal scholars, even those like al-Awza'i who contributed to the development of laws of war and the frontier, were peripheral and could be ignored. This contrast is a reminder that the chronicles alone are not sufficient for the reconstruction of early Islamic history.

The state of the sources for the study of early Islamic history generally, and for an attempt to reconstruct the life and thought of al-Awza'i specifically, is somewhat problematic, but not altogether hopeless. The limitations of the sources are daunting. There is no archive. Most of al-Awza'i's writings are lost and the fragments that survive present obvious challenges. For whatever reason, al-Awza'i's students were less prolific in their writing than were students of his rivals. Despite his apparently good relationship with Christians in his community, non-Muslim sources do not mention al-Awza'i at all. Everything that is known about him derives from later sources, some of which were hostile to him.

Despite all of this, the situation is not as bleak as it could be. Traces of al-Awza'i's thoughts and deeds can be found in a wide range of sources. Legal scholars cited him. Biographers memorialized him with varying degrees of detail. Other sources mention him as well. The material that does survive offers differing perspectives on al-Awza'i. Almost none of it was written by acolytes praising their master. Conversely, while some works were intended to refute him, most were not.

There are, in fact, certain advantages to be found in the assorted, fragmentary sources on al-Awza'i. Arguably, a clearer image of him can be drawn from these fragments than could be provided by a single, detailed, fawning hagiography by one of his pupils. The fact that the sources display a strong degree of consistency in recording al-Awza'i's legal opinions and religious views is particularly striking. This consistency implies that later scholars drew on some corpus of material about al-Awza'i that preserved his views, or at the very least that there was near universal agreement about what al-Awza'i thought about a variety of major issues. This in itself is significant. The fact that scholars persisted in recording al-Awza'i's views, despite the fact that he had no following and had produced no legal texts that merited preservation or commentary, underscores al-Awza'i's importance as a scholar and as an example of past Islamic jurisprudence.

Any reconstruction of al-Awza'i's life and work must be based on fragments and traces of his thought and cannot provide a complete, definitive image of the man and his influence. Given his prominence during the Umayyad period, when Islamic law was in its formative era, along with the continued interest later Muslim scholars devoted to him, it is still important to scour the sources carefully and thoroughly to gain a better, albeit incomplete, understanding of al-Awza'i.

2

AL-AWZA'I'S JURISPRUDENCE

Despite the fact that he had broader intellectual interests and political ambitions, al-Awza'i is primarily remembered as a jurist (faqih).
However, his prominence as a theologian, discussed in chapter 4, was
considerable, and he enjoyed access to the most powerful Umayyad
political circles. In addition, the sources note his acumen as a muhaddith. For reasons that will be discussed below, all of these aspects of
al-Awza'i's influence are overshadowed by his contributions to Islamic
law, despite the apparent modesty of his long-term legal impact.

LAW IN THE FORMATIVE PERIOD OF ISLAM

The trajectory of early Islamic legal formation was long, complex, and
ultimately very poorly documented. While it is beyond the scope of
this work to offer a comprehensive discussion of the process of Islamic
legal development, a general outline of the field and its early trends is
essential for understanding al-Awza'i's work and its influence.

Unfortunately, available sources make it difficult to assess the process by which Islamic law developed, or even who made particular
contributions to the field. Legal sources in general suffer from the
same limitations discussed in the previous chapter. Little from the
earliest period has survived and what has survived is preserved sec-
ond-hand in later legal works. For Muslim scholars in the early Islamic
centuries, the gaps in the legal sources were a particularly urgent problem. Minor inconsistencies in sources for other fields were vexing,
but not necessarily disastrous. Contradictory historical chronologies,

discrepancies about who led particular expeditions, and disputed attri-
butions of bits of poetry were certainly annoying, and sorting out such
problems consumed much time and discussion. However, confusion
over legal sources could have dire consequences. Knowing what God
commanded and forbade was crucial. Mistakes about such matters
could have severe implications, both for one's terrestrial life and for
one's eternal status. Hence, the effort to find correct answers and to
fill in gaps in the sources was intensive, contentious, and urgent. The
faithful required legal clarity in order to conform their behavior to
God's demands.

The desire for definitive answers to legal questions inspired extensive scholarly efforts to find sources and define methods to determine
what the law was. During the first/seventh and second/eighth centuries, the volume of legal sources, particularly *hadith*, grew expo-
nentially. From the beginning, the growth in legal material inspired
questions about the authenticity of newly found *hadith* and other
sources. Scholars sometimes endured accusations of fabricating prophetic *hadith* to defend particular views. More often, there was uncertainty about the veracity of sources, and concerns that scholars placed
too much confidence in tenuous recollections of the past. These initial
debates about the reliability of the sources, their meaning, and their
authenticity have continued in various forms, with shifting vocabulary
and methods, until modern times.

The discussion of early Islamic law and the sources informing it was
divided into two separate, but at times overlapping, categories: the
usul al-fiqh and the *furu' al-fiqh*. *Usul al-fiqh*, or roots of jurisprudence,
is roughly equivalent to modern notions of legal theory. It focuses on
how one determines what the law is, what sources are acceptable as
legal foundations, and what methods one may use to interpret them.
In short, *usul al-fiqh* centers on how to find the rules. *Furu' al-fiqh*,
or branches of jurisprudence, involves the actual rules derived via
the *usul*, similar to modern notions of positive law. In the *furu'*, one
finds practical answers to everyday legal questions and instruction for
Muslims about how to behave. For most Muslims, especially non-ju-
rists, the *furu'* was the more important category. They cared more
about what the rules were than about complex explanations regarding

their derivation. As the discussion below will demonstrate, this need for specific instruction about proper behavior affected the nature and volume of sources that have been preserved.

For legal scholars like al-Awza'i and his contemporaries, however, the roots were as important as the branches, and disagreements about how to derive the law could be intense. In al-Awza'i's time, the proper methods for deriving the law remained contested. To some extent, that remains the case even in modern times. Essentially, arguments about the proper derivation of Islamic law revolved around three constellations of legal sources: the Qur'an, exemplary past practice, and an assortment of forms of reasoning and logic. The Qur'an's legal pronouncements are sometimes explicit, but more often vague and even apparently contradictory. While Muslim scholars rarely question the legal authority of God's revelation, the Qur'an itself hardly offers a complete, comprehensive legal code. Quasi-revelatory statements from the Prophet (hadith qudsi) do not add enough to derive law exclusively from statements from the divine.

A second constellation of sources looks to examples from past practice as legally normative. Whose past practice can be consulted is the subject of intense debate. Obviously, the Prophet himself can be considered as an exemplar, though his fallibility is also acknowledged. Some scholars broaden the circle of exemplars to include the Prophet's companions and pious members of the following generation. A few scholars accept past community practice and customs as normative as well. In addition to debate about whose practices can be considered sources of law, there is even greater disagreement about how to determine what these potential exemplars' practice actually was. Sources describing the actions and moral choices of the Prophet and other pious individuals and groups are both voluminous and filled with contradictions and confusion.

The third category of sources involves human reasoning of several sorts. Legal scholars applied various logical methods to address contradictions and to derive answers based on sparse sources. These methods range from complex analogies and syllogisms steeped in Aristotelian thought and vocabulary to simple commonsense reasoning. Naturally, there were intensive debates about which methods could be applied to

Islamic law as well as about the validity of specific logical arguments and proofs.

For legal experts, this distillation of Islamic legal sources into three broad categories may seem too simplistic. However, it captures the general state of jurisprudence during the early period. There was no consensus about the parameters of any of these three source constellations, nor about how sources within each category should be used. The relationship between different types of legal sources inspired more contentious debates, some of which continue today. Could the Prophet's practice overrule Qur'anic revelation? Should choices the Prophet and early community made be discarded because they were illogical, or even inexplicable? Could contemporary circumstances and knowledge render earlier practices obsolete? Were certain types of sources even valid to begin with, regardless of their content or context?

In al-Awza'i's time, these debates were beginning, though they were still very much in an embryonic phase. Distinct schools of thought were only starting to emerge and the boundaries between them were amorphous at best. Even the vocabulary used to describe particular sources, especially the application of reasoning, was not yet consistent, making it difficult to discern the fault lines that separated jurists and inspired sometimes fierce competition and animosity between them.

The embryonic status of *usul al-fiqh* did not reduce the demand for *furu'* during al-Awza'i's time. Believers needed answers to practical legal questions more than they needed coherent legal theories. The legal guidance provided by the *furu'* was broader than modern notions of law. It extended beyond what now would be considered criminal and civil law to include rules about ritual and liturgical practices as well. As a consequence of this immediate need for answers, more of the early material that survives or has been reproduced in later works is related to the *furu'* than to the *usul*.

In particular, the *ikhtilaf* literature preserves a rich variety of purportedly early *furu'* material. These works are repositories documenting disagreements between legal scholars about a wide array of topics. While these works were mostly written later — the earliest

dates from the late third/ninth century – they focus on disagreements
between scholars of earlier generations. The questions addressed are
quite diverse and often entail legal and ritual minutiae, devoting long
discussions to topics such as how to determine if water is clean enough
for ablutions or how many pebbles one should use as a substitute to
perform ablutions in the absence of clean water. The broad spectrum
these works cover is a reminder that, even in the earliest period,
Islamic law reached into all aspects of a believer's life.

The *ikhtilaf* works seldom include extensive explanations of the reasoning behind scholars' views on particular questions. This was not
their purpose. Instead, these works provided catalogues of answers
to practical legal questions and satisfied the needs of believers more
concerned with what they should do in particular situations than with
the nuances of legal theory. Where the *ikhtilaf* works do address *usul*,
their explanations at times appear to be retrofitted, using vocabulary
and reasoning that were not part of the discourse of the early scholars
whose opinions they list. At times, this appears to be an effort to confront confusion and inconsistencies in the answers scholars offered. At
times, it seems to reflect the later need for answers to appear to be
systematic rather than ad hoc. Understanding the limitations of these
sources is important for the discussion of al-Awza'i that follows. To an
extent, his role in the development of Islamic law has been retrofitted
by later authors of *ikhtilaf* and other works. Efforts to find his actual
influence require an awareness of the layers of interpretation and reinterpretations of his thought that must be peeled back to approximate
his actual role.

AL-AWZA'I'S FIQH

The legal landscape during al-Awza'i's time was not yet clearly
defined. A variety of paradigms were employed by later Muslim legal
scholars and eventually by modern scholars to describe the emergence
of legal factions and divisions in early Islam, but the situation remained
fluid for at least a century after al-Awza'i's death. As the organizational schemes for describing differing schools of law developed,

scholars tried to find appropriate ways to categorize early figures like al-Awza'i, whose followers were no longer numerous enough to participate in this discourse.

Ultimately, legal *madhhabs* (schools) were defined as followers of particular early legal scholars who served as eponyms if not founders of these *madhhabs*. It is not always clear whether the legal approaches ascribed to a particular eponym were his own, or were elaborations from his students, seeking to systemize their mentor's approach. For the surviving *madhhabs*, a growing and complex literature eventually emerged detailing the schools' positions on both theoretical and practical matters. For scholars like al-Awza'i, whose followers dwindled rapidly, this process of systemization and explication was aborted. Despite this, there are examples in later legal literature, and certainly in modern studies, wherein a distinctly al-Awza'i *madhhab* is assumed to have existed. Unfortunately, his followers' literary output was virtually nonexistent, or perhaps simply lost. Consequently, details of his theoretical views are especially scarce.

In addition to, perhaps prior to, the eponymous model, Islamic legal approaches were often described regionally. Reports often note differences between Syrian, Iraqi, and Hijazi (Medinan) solutions to legal and ritual questions, suggesting that there were distinctly regional approaches to Islamic law, presumably built on the customary practices of local inhabitants or developed from the preferences of the earliest Islamic leaders in those places. In this organizational scheme, al-Awza'i serves as the most prominent representative of the Syrian school of thought, along with Makhul al-Shami (d. *c*. 113/731) and Ibn Shihab al-Zuhri (d. 124/742), whose views he sometimes cites.

Finally, the earliest theoretical rift between Islamic legal scholars separated them into two factions, the *ashab al-ra'y* (partisans of personal opinion) and the *ahl al-hadith* (*hadith* folk). The *ashab al-ra'y* appear to have been geographically concentrated in Iraq, more specifically in Kufa. They advocated the application of logical methods, analogy, and personal reasoning to legal questions and sought to ensure that answers to legal questions were logically consistent. Their opponents, the *ahl al-hadith*, who were not always closely associated with a particular locale, relied instead on the example of the Prophet as a

major source for legal precedents. In this division, al-Awza'i is generally assigned to the *ahl al-hadith*, though this association is largely by
default. His ongoing feud with prominent advocates of *ra'y*, discussed
in more detail below, led to his categorization as part of the *ahl al-
hadith*. The fact that he did not often rely on *hadith* in his legal rulings
does not seem to have mattered a great deal to those sorting scholars
into factions.

In the later legal sources utilized in this study, these three categorization schemes comingle. At times there are references to the views
of the *ashab al-ra'y* as though they were a distinct group. At other
times, the same scholars are defined as Kufans or Iraqis instead. In
other instances, views are attached to followers of the eponyms of
later schools. Occasionally, multiple classification schemes appear
adjacent to each other in the responses to individual questions in the
ikhtilaf sources. All of this serves as evidence that the sorting of scholars by eponymous, regional, or methodological *madhhab*s came later
and that these classifications were grafted onto earlier debates.

In the legal literature that survives, al-Awza'i appears as a representative of several legal factions. At times, he is described as the eponym
of his own legal *madhhab*. At other times, he is the spokesman for
the Syrian school. In some instances, he acts as a *muhaddith*, refuting
the *ashab al-ra'y*. Curiously, nowhere in the sources examined does
al-Awza'i appear as the representative of Umayyad solutions to legal
questions. Despite his association with the Umayyad regime and his
prominence as a legal adviser at the caliph's court, later sources largely
ignore this aspect of his career. His separation from the Umayyads in
these sources is significant in that it may suggest that later scholars
tried to rehabilitate him by disassociating him from his patrons. If this
is the case, it provides strong evidence that the *ikhtilaf* authors and
others were not merely compiling views of earlier authorities, but
that they were exercising a heavier editorial hand to remove the taint
of early authorities' questionable associations.

As discussed in the previous chapter, no *usul al-fiqh* texts from
al-Awza'i survive. It is doubtful that he wrote any theoretical works
of jurisprudence, focusing his attention instead on practical questions.
In this he was not unusual. By and large, the legal luminaries of his

generation did not write theoretical works. In fact, they wrote very little on any topic. The closest approximation to a legal text written by one of al-Awza'i's contemporaries is Malik's *Muwatta'*, which is actually better described as an annotated collection of *hadith* than as a theoretical work of jurisprudence. The only works by al-Awza'i's rival Abu Hanifa that survive are short creedal statements rather than legal texts. Later generations of students of these great thinkers were far more prolific than their masters. For instance, Sahnun's (d. 240/854) *Mudawwana*, written two generations after Malik's death, provides a far more comprehensive collection of Malik's statements and explanations of his reasoning than did his own work, the *Muwatta'*. Similarly, most of what is preserved from Abu Hanifa comes from the works of his students, Abu Yusuf (d. 182/798), al-Shaybani (d. 189/805), and others.

Al-Awza'i was consistent with his contemporaries in his failure, or perhaps reluctance, to write a comprehensive work of legal theory. Unlike his contemporaries, however, al-Awza'i's students did not take up the task of explicating their master's legal thought in more theoretical works. One can only speculate about the reasons for their lack of literary production. The most plausible explanation is that the fall of the Umayyad dynasty hampered al-Awza'i's ability to cultivate a new generation of acolytes. Regardless of the causes, the consequence is that modern scholars cannot turn to theoretical texts written by followers of al-Awza'i to understand his jurisprudence. Instead, it is necessary to turn to later *furu'* works to try to glean legal method from examples of practical legal pronouncements. In some cases, the legal reasoning behind al-Awza'i's opinion on a particular question is obvious in his answer. In other instances, his theoretical approach is harder, or even impossible to ferret out from the material preserved. A few examples will illustrate both the potential and limitations of these sources for reconstructing al-Awza'i's thought.

There are numerous instances in the *ikhtilaf* and *siyar* works where al-Awza'i invokes the practice of the Prophet. Most of these do not entail formal citations of prophetic *hadith*, complete with *isnads*, but instead simply state what the Prophet did in particular situations. Al-Awza'i typically either states definitively what the Prophet did, or asserts, perhaps less confidently, that he heard that the Prophet made a particular choice. These appeals to prophetic example tend to focus on questions of warfare and spoils, using the Prophet's decisions during and after battles at Uhud, Khaybar, and Mecca as precedents.

In some cases, al-Awzaʿiʾs use of prophetic example is coupled with rudimentary analogy to reach a conclusion. For instance, his student al-Fazari reports in his *Kitab al-siyar* that he asked al-Awzaʿi about tomb desecration. Al-Awzaʿi responded that this was an evil deed. He then offered a *hadith* (with a partial *isnad*) in which the Prophet forbade entry into the houses of dead enemies. Al-Awzaʿi then asked rhetorically, if the Prophet forbade entry into their houses, how could entry to their tombs be allowed? Here al-Awzaʿi begins with a prophetic *hadith* and expands the scope of the Prophet's admonition by implying that the sanctity of a tomb exceeds that of a house, therefore making entry even more reprehensible. While al-Awzaʿi does not present a formal analogy or explain his reasoning particularly thoroughly, the analogy is obvious.

Al-Fazari presents other examples in which al-Awzaʿi employs more explicit analogies. For instance, he determines that a lynx that is captured should not be divided with the spoils because it is like a dog and must therefore be excluded. Ibn ʿAbd al-Barr (d. 423/1071) reports that, for tax purposes, al-Awzaʿi joined other scholars in treating dates, olives, and grapes as fruit while categorizing barley and sorghum as wheat. He also agreed that in preparation for prayer, one should wipe one's turban in the same manner as one's legs. Here Ibn ʿAbd al-Barr describes al-Awzaʿiʾs reasoning explicitly as *qiyas*, the technical term for analogy. However, this choice of vocabulary appears to be Ibn ʿAbd al-Barrʾs rather than al-Awzaʿiʾs.

In addition to explicit and implicit use of analogy, citations of al-Awzaʿi frequently invoke past practice. He mentions the actions of various companions of the Prophet as precedents, as well as decisions made by later caliphs, including ʿUmar b. ʿAbd al-ʿAziz (r. 99/717–101/720) in particular. He also cites opinions of earlier generations of scholars, such as al-Zuhri and Makhul al-Shami, without providing any explanation of their reasoning.

In a surprising number of cases, al-Awzaʿi explicitly states his own personal opinion without offering any rationale whatsoever. For example, al-Fazari presented al-Awza'i with a hypothetical case in which a Muslim soldier had been captured and was about to be executed. The condemned man suggested that the executioner behead him with his own sword because it was sharper than the executioner's and would provide a less painful demise. Al-Awza'i simply responded, "This does not please me." In another example, al-Fazari asks al-Awza'i whether Greek books found in conquered territory should be burned or sold. Al-Awza'i responds that he would prefer that they be buried instead. In these and many other cases, al-Awza'i's answers to legal queries clearly involve personal preferences and he provides no supporting explanation for his opinions.

Other examples address more complicated questions and create some confusion about al-Awza'i's methods. A significant portion of the material attributed to al-Awza'i in the *siyar* works deals with issues surrounding theft from spoils taken in battle. The evaluation, monetization, and distribution of spoils is inherently tedious and exceptions and peculiar situations abound. Theft from spoils appears to have been a frequent occurrence, made more complex by the fact that in some cases borrowing from the spoils was acceptable. Al-Awza'i's explanation of the punishment meted out to someone caught stealing from the spoils illustrates both some of the complexities of the problem and some of the difficulty in making sense of al-Awza'i's methods. His exchange with al-Fazari about the issue, reported in his *Kitab al-siyar*, is instructive.

> Al-Fazari: I asked al-Awza'i about theft from the spoils (*ghulul*). I asked: Is the punishment the same regardless of whether the theft is small or large?
> Al-Awza'i: It is the same.
> Al-Fazari: Is that which was stolen burned?
> Al-Awza'i: No.
> Al-Fazari: Are the thief's possessions burned?
> Al-Awza'i: Yes.
> Al-Fazari: Are the shares of the spoils assigned to him burned?
> Al-Awza'i: Yes.
> Al-Fazari: And the shares assigned to his horse? Are they burned?
> Al-Awza'i: Yes. He receives nothing at all from the campaign. The commander (*imam*) sees to his punishment.

Al-Fazari: What if he has already squandered what he stole?

Al-Awza'i: The commander imposes a fine upon him and burns his possessions.

Al-Fazari: And what part of his possessions are to be burned?

Al-Awza'i: Everything he has brought with him on campaign, including his saddle (sarj) and saddle pad (ikaf).

Al-Fazari: And his horses? And the provisions in his saddlebag?

Al-Awza'i: No.

Al-Fazari: Is his armor burned?

Al-Awza'i: No. Nor is the robe he is wearing.

Al-Fazari: What is your opinion about items of his possessions that are put in the fire and do not burn because they are made of metal or the like? Can someone take them?

Al-Awza'i: No. The punishment is the fire. Whatever survives, its owner has a right to retrieve.

Al-Fazari: What if a man steals from the spoils and is not caught until he returns home and then the theft is discovered? Are the possessions in his home burned, or just those he took with him on campaign?

Al-Awza'i: Only the possessions he took on campaign.

Al-Fazari: What if the thief dies and then his theft is discovered? Are his possessions burned?

Al-Awza'i: No. Because the Prophet did not burn the possessions of a thief whose theft was discovered after he died.

The discussion continues with more hypothetical scenarios before turning to even more complicated possibilities, such as how to deal with a slave who steals from the spoils. This dialogue illustrates the difficulties involved in uncovering al-Awza'i's legal reasoning. He cites no sources for most of his conclusions. His assertion about prophetic practice at the end of the excerpt does not reference a particular *hadith* report, and nor does a report to this effect appear in any of the standard *hadith* collections. Al-Awza'i also offers no rationale for the distinctions he makes. For instance, why is a thief's saddle burned, but not his armor? Why is he allowed to retain his saddlebag and retrieve items that do not burn? Any attempt to find the underlying logic of al-Awza'i's answers must be largely speculative. It is possible that those for whom these answers were provided had some knowledge of the reasons for the distinctions al-Awza'i makes, or that answers could be found in lost texts. For modern scholars, however, given the data available, al-Awza'i's reasoning is often elusive.

Examples from *furu'* texts still remain useful for reconstructing al-Awza'i's legal thought, however. They show that he relied on a variety of methods to derive legal rulings. In some cases, he appeals to scripture or to prophetic example, albeit often without the formal documentation of *hadith* upon which later generations would insist. He does make explicit and implicit references to community prac- tice and to the example of pious figures of earlier generations. There are also ample examples of reasoning by analogy, though without the technical Aristotelian syllogistic vocabulary that later scholars would employ. In many other cases, al-Awza'i simply declares his opinion, apparently with the expectation that his own authority would be suf- ficient. While these examples offer no real discussion of legal the- ory, they do illustrate that al-Awza'i did not limit himself to a single source or type of source for his legal rulings. Unfortunately, they do not clearly demonstrate which of the various sources and methods he used took priority over the others.

While it is perhaps unsatisfying to find so little evidence of method in al-Awza'i's rulings, it is important to remember that this is not atypical for his era. Other legal scholars were similarly cryptic in their pronouncements as well, providing answers to questions without elaborating much on theory. As discussed above, later generations of scholars explicated, or perhaps even created, the theory behind their mentors' legal declarations. By examining a sufficient corpus of the *furu'* texts, one can begin to see patterns in al-Awza'i's responses by tracing the frequency with which he appeals to particular sources or methods and contrasting his explanations to those of other scholars. This type of analysis can suggest which of al-Awza'i's multiple meth- ods for deriving law was his preferred approach. However, limitations remain. For example, it is possible that in cases where al-Awza'i relies on analogy he may have preferred to be able to cite past practice, but no examples were known to him. Or, in other cases, what appears to be a simple declaration of opinion may implicitly refer to a *hadith* report his contemporaries would have been expected to know, but which is now lost or obscure. Despite these limitations, al-Awza'i's responses to specific legal questions can provide a broad outline of his approach to legal theory.

Relying on such material, Joseph Schacht offered the first modern interpretation of al-Awza'i's jurisprudence some sixty years ago. He argued that al-Awza'i's solutions to legal questions represented some of the earliest understandings of Islamic law. He added that al-Awza'i articulated a "living tradition" based on an evolving set of community practices. Schacht further suggested that al-Awza'i and other early scholars represented a "common ancient doctrine" of law that only later evolved into more orderly, theory-grounded systems.

Despite the limited sources at Schacht's disposal, his interpretation still has merit. Al-Awza'i's solutions do appear to have been among the earliest to many legal questions, perhaps explaining in part why he so seldom explicitly cited his predecessors. However, he was not the only early scholar offering legal opinions. Nor were early legal scholars in agreement about a common doctrine or approach to legal issues of any kind. Indeed, even a tentative perusal of the *ikhtilaf* works demonstrates frequent disagreements between scholars of al-Awza'i's generation. An examination of a broader array of sources also reveals that al-Awza'i relied less frequently on the so-called living tradition than Schacht's data suggested.

Based on an analysis of citations of al-Awza'i in *furu'* works, specifically *ikhtilaf* and *siyar* texts, a general understanding of his preferred methods can be tentatively reached. More detailed analyses can be found elsewhere. A less tedious summary will suffice here. As alluded to above, al-Awza'i used a variety of methods to derive legal opinions and did not rely exclusively, or even predominantly, on a particular mode of reasoning. The sources also seldom include any explanation of his thought process. This is not unusual. It is a product of the nature of the sources and the state of legal discourse during his era.

Few of the opinions al-Awza'i offers include specific references to the Qur'an or to prophetic *hadith*. Nor are invocations of other past authorities particularly numerous. Al-Awza'i does occasionally mention past exemplars in his responses. He also cites his own teachers, though not often and usually without further explanation. Similarly, appeals to custom or traditional community practice are not prevalent.

Somewhat surprisingly, al-Awza'i specifically acknowledges that he is stating his own opinion fairly frequently, beginning responses with phrases like "I think," or "I prefer." In fact, these explicit statements of personal opinion appear more frequently than do prophetic *hadith*. As some of the examples cited above illustrate, more often than not, al-Awza'i simply makes declarative statements about legal questions with no explanation of his reasoning. In many cases, these answers are a simple "yes" or "no."

Defining al-Awza'i's approach to *usul al-fiqh* based on such evidence is difficult and a bit unsatisfying. At best, the result is a series of negative conclusions. Al-Awza'i did not rely heavily on *hadith*. Nor did he explicitly privilege past practice or some sort of living tradition. He relied on logic and his own opinion more often than Schacht suggested, but not exclusively. Al-Awza'i's connection to the *ahl al-hadith* is clearly a later accretion, given the extent to which he relies on logic instead of *hadith*. His identification with a Syrian regional school is also tentative, given how infrequently this association actually appears in the sources.

Al-Awza'i's approach to legal questions is often marked by practicality and flexibility. He is typically deferential to political authorities, particularly on the frontier and in combat zones. He also regularly accepts necessity as a justification for his rulings. The vocabulary of his appeals to necessity is worth noting. Typically, al-Awza'i uses the term *darura* to connote necessity, rather than terms like *istislah*, *istihsan*, or *maslaha*, terms more commonly used in early texts to refer to upholding the public good. *Darura*, by contrast did not become a standard legal term until much later, sometime after the texts used here were compiled. Whether the term had an archaic phase, represented by al-Awza'i, is an interesting question that merits further discussion. The peculiar terminology is also a reminder of how fluid legal concepts and their signifiers remained during the early Islamic period. Of course, it is also important to note that the fluidity of terminology and diversity of methods displayed in al-Awza'i's *fiqh* were not unusual. The same uncertainty can be found in the legal pronouncements of his contemporaries as well.

Despite the methodological state of flux during al-Awza'i's time, scholars were still expected to produce definitive answers to specific

legal questions. Typically, even when scholars did not explain themselves, they did stubbornly maintain their chosen positions on particular issues. Based on the available sources, it is possible to reconstruct
at least the broad outlines of al-Awza'i's positive law.

Later scholars, and modern scholars in particular, tended to treat
al-Awza'i primarily as an expert on the laws of war and on legal issues
related to the frontier. His long residence in Beirut, which was considered a frontier base at the time, may have contributed to this impression. The preservation of portions of his *Kitab al-siyar* was certainly
a factor as well, as was the fact that issues related to warfare, spoils,
and the disposition of conquered lands were especially important to
the political elites of both the Umayyad and early Abbasid periods.
His conflicts with Abu Hanifa and his student Abu Yusuf about these
issues reflect their relevance as well, and may have contributed to al-
Awza'i's reputation as a frontier expert.

Despite the prominence of frontier issues in discussions of al-
Awza'i, these topics actually constituted a small part of his legal output. The *ikhtilaf* works preserve material from al-Awza'i touching
on all aspects of Islamic law. In fact, they include more citations of
al-Awza'i's opinions about non-political topics involving prayer and
ritual than about warfare. To understand al-Awza'i's approach to positive law, it is essential to look at a broader collection of topics than
the *siyar*.

However, because the laws of war are the focus of so much research
about al-Awza'i, it is reasonable to begin with the *siyar*. This is an
area of law that was the focus of significant disagreements during al-
Awza'i's time, and one that had significant financial and other implications. The fact that rivals reproduced portions of al-Awza'i's *Kitab
al-siyar* and engaged in debate over his conclusions underscores both
the importance of the topic and the influence of al-Awza'i's views.

One area of disagreement focused on the distribution of extra
shares of spoils to horsemen. There was universal agreement that
horsemen should be rewarded more than foot soldiers, presumably
to compensate for the cost of maintaining their mounts. The dispute
was over how much more they should receive. Al-Awza'i, whose view
was followed by most other scholars, held that the horseman received

one share for himself and two for his horse, for a total of three shares. Abu Hanifa disagreed, calling for the horseman to receive a share for himself and one for his horse, two shares in total. He held this position despite a *hadith* report to the contrary. He defended his view by objecting to the idea that a horse should be compensated more than a human. How could a horse merit twice the reward assigned to a believing Muslim soldier? Interestingly, in his refutation of al-Awza'i, Abu Yusuf did not jump to defend his master's views, but merely reported the two opinions. He did, however, attack al-Awza'i on another ancillary aspect of this debate. Scholars, and likely wealthy horsemen, needed to know if a horseman could collect shares for more than one horse. Al-Awza'i held that a horseman could collect shares for a second horse, but not a third, producing a maximum of five shares for a horseman, regardless of how many additional horses he brought to the frontier. Abu Yusuf mocked al-Awza'i's position, essentially asking how he came to the number two, rather than three, or four, etc. While Abu Hanifa's rationale for ignoring *hadith* was perhaps dubious, al-Awza'i's explanation for limiting shares to two horses is never provided. Incidentally, shares for horses was apparently a contentious question, as the *siyar* literature includes many queries about such matters. There was much discussion about whether lame horses or nags received shares. Al-Awza'i was generous in this regard. There were even questions about whether someone who brought his horse on board a ship for a naval battle received shares for the horse. Again, al-Awza'i was amenable to providing for the horse, even though its usefulness in naval combat was likely to have been negligible.

On other matters, al-Awza'i stands out for insisting that *dhimmi*s (non-Muslim subjects) who fought alongside Muslims should receive shares of the spoils. Other authorities rejected this view. He also held that merchants and scribes who joined combat should receive shares, but that craftsmen and donkey drivers should not. He emphasized that it was virtuous to provide gifts to those who fought but were not entitled to shares, following the example of the Prophet. Many of the questions al-Awza'i addresses regarding warfare and spoils involve minutiae that are not discussed by other scholars. On the one hand, this makes it difficult to compare his views and approach to others.

On the other hand, the fact that his, and only his, responses to so
many detailed questions have been preserved underscores al-Awza'i's
authority on such matters.

Little has been preserved about al-Awza'i's views on issues of taxation and land tenure. This is somewhat surprising, given his close
association with government circles and the obvious importance of
taxation policies to any political regime. Al-Awza'i does report a
number of prophetic *hadith* in which the Prophet frowns upon rent-
ing land and offers contradictory opinions regarding sharecropping.
However, al-Awza'i's own views on these matters are not recorded.
He did disagree with Abu Hanifa regarding the fiscally significant question of whether *kharaj* land purchased by a Muslim remained subject
to the *jizya* tax. Al-Awza'i held that the tax no longer applied, which
would have had significant consequences for the treasury. He also forbade Muslims from profiting from interest-bearing loans while in non-
Muslim territory, even though he allowed some other rules of Islamic
law to be suspended there.

In regards to *zakat*, the required alms-giving for Muslims that
functioned essentially as a form of taxation, al-Awza'i disagreed with
others about certain details, but a clear pattern cannot be detected.
For instance, he allowed debtors to exempt what they owed from
the calculation of the base amount to which *zakat* applied. On the
other hand, he exempted less of one's net worth from the calculation.
Hence, he appears to be neither more lenient nor more stringent in
his calculations. He also disagreed with others about the application
of *zakat* to certain goods, making distinctions between irrigated and
non-irrigated orchards and applying the tax to pasturing livestock but
not to draft animals. Here again, it is difficult to find broad patterns.
Disagreements about *zakat* appear to involve minutiae rather than
major principles.

Al-Awza'i also devoted a considerable amount of attention to
issues involving prayer and ritual. In fact, the *ikhtilaf* sources include
far more material from al-Awza'i regarding these matters than that
addressing warfare issues. His attention to ritual underscores the
breadth of his legal acumen and is a reminder that he was not merely a
frontier scholar. His interest in ritual is also significant because this is

an area that was largely outside politics. Given al-Awza'i's association with the Umayyad caliphs, it is tempting to see him as a scholar concerned primarily with the kinds of governmental issues about which his patrons needed advice. Instead, al-Awza'i expressed his views on virtually every aspect of Islamic law.

It is difficult to characterize any legal scholar's views on prayer and ritual, or to argue for a distinct approach attached to a particular *madhhab*. The focus is often on details and here, more than in other areas of law, guidance is sought from the precedents set by the Prophet and the early community. When theory is lacking, example becomes crucial. Eventually, certain gestures or sequences of gestures come to be associated with different sectarian groups, serving as symbols of affiliation. However, during al-Awza'i's time, such subtlety does not appear to have gained significant meaning.

While a specifically "al-Awza'i" ritual practice cannot be identified, an examination of his statements about prayer and ritual purity suggests that, in general, he was more lenient regarding details than were some of his contemporaries. In contrast to others, he did not require that ablutions be repeated if someone found dried blood on himself or his clothing (though uncoagulated blood still required one to repeat one's ablutions). He also allowed a man to touch his wife, though not other women, without negating his state of ritual cleanliness. Men and women could also share ablution water in the same vessel without negative consequences.

Al-Awza'i was also less strict regarding some aspects of conduct during prayer. For instance, he considered it acceptable for worshipers to greet each other during prayer and to bless someone who sneezed during the proceedings. He also allowed people to stand and walk about during the Friday sermon (*khutba*), so long as they did not block the aisle or talk. Al-Awza'i considered some pauses during prayer to be optional and allowed minor elements to be omitted. In general, he was less concerned with precise motions and behaviors during prayer than were some of his contemporaries. He was also more lenient regarding who could lead the prayers. He agreed with his colleagues that it was acceptable to pray behind a ritually impure *imam*. However, he went further and saw no problem with prayers being led by an *imam* who was the product of adultery. In the absence of an *imam*, al-Awza'i held that the most knowledgeable man present should lead prayers.

While these examples suggest a degree of flexibility in al-Awza'i's attitudes toward prayer, there were other aspects of prayer about which he was especially strict. He was adamant that the opening *fatiha* could never be omitted from prayer. He also insisted that funeral services conclude before the *'asr* (afternoon) prayer. Others were more flexible about the timing and length of funeral prayers. Al-Awza'i was also more stringent in his attitude toward shortening prayers during travel. While he does not say so explicitly, one gets the sense that he suspected that some used travel as an excuse to shirk their required prayers. Curiously, while he does not expound much upon details of specific motions during prayer, Ibn 'Abd al-Barr includes one report in which he criticizes the Kufans for not raising their hands high enough at certain points, a practice that in his mind diminished the efficacy of their prayers. This is also one of the rare regional references al-Awza'i makes.

The few hundred citations of al-Awza'i's responses to narrow ritual questions are not sufficient for drawing more than a very general conclusion about his attitude toward prayer and ritual. He seems to have focused on practicality and to have been relatively forgiving toward errors and omissions in prayers. This stance is consistent with the fluidity of the development of ritual practices during the period and may also reflect informalities that frontier life imposed. In some instances, al-Awza'i bases his responses to questions about prayer on the practice of the Prophet or of later exemplars. This is to be expected, since ritual motion largely involves emulation of pious guides. There are occasionally hints of a Syrian way of praying, though these are rare. More often than not, al-Awza'i simply states his views, assuming that his audience will accept his authority.

EVALUATING AL-AWZA'I AS A LEGAL SCHOLAR

The discussions above have illustrated how difficult it is to find a clearly articulated approach to *fiqh* in the materials about al-Awza'i that have survived. His legal responses include few references to Qur'an and *hadith*. He occasionally invokes past practice of the community as a source of guidance. There are also examples where the lack of past practice serves as precedent. In response to hypothetical questions, al-Awza'i occasionally responds by saying that he has never heard of anyone doing certain things. In a few cases, he even acknowledges that he does not know anything about the issue at hand. These responses are especially significant because they indicate that in the many instances in which al-Awza'i simply declares an answer, he is basing it on something he has learned and is not merely stating his opinion. Al-Awza'i regularly uses analogies of various sorts, but is not explicit and never employs the technical vocabulary that later scholars adopted. There are also indications that he was prone to allow the *amir* or *imam* (terms often used interchangeably) wide discretion.

While this vague description of al-Awza'i's approach to jurisprudence is not entirely satisfying, it is important to remember that other scholars' *madhhabs* were in a similar state during al-Awza'i's era. Without later school texts, the Maliki and Hanafi *madhhabs'* doctrines would be equally opaque. It is also important to recognize that the sources that preserve material on al-Awza'i's *fiqh*, particularly the *ikhtilaf* works, are not works of legal theory, but catalogues of decisions often bereft of explanation.

Both modern and medieval scholars have at times tried to categorize al-Awza'i's *fiqh*, though their conclusions have not been entirely convincing. Often, al-Awza'i is treated as a representative, or even leader, of a Syrian *madhhab*. This categorization is compatible with the widely accepted teleology, wherein legal development evolves from ad hoc solutions to regional schools to eponymous *madhhabs*. Under this model, al-Awza'i falls in the transition between regional and eponymous and is therefore associated with his Syrian geography. There are problems with the model in general, which are beyond the scope of this discussion. More important, the evidence from actual reports does not support al-Awza'i's definition as a representative of Syrian *fiqh*. He rarely refers to Syrian practice, and there is no regional pattern to his agreements and disagreements with other scholars. In addition, his students and associates hailed from all over the Muslim world, demonstrating his broader appeal.

Joseph Schacht's conclusion that al-Awza'i represented a common ancient doctrine has been widely accepted as well. While al-Awza'i certainly represents early solutions to Islamic legal questions, simply because he was an early scholar, there is little indication of early consensus on even the most basic of questions. Instead, his generation disagreed about many crucial issues. The evidence in the *ikhtilaf* literature suggests that there was no common doctrine, and nor were there clearly defined factions of jurists who approached problems in a similar manner.

Instead, al-Awza'i appears to have been one of many early Islamic legal scholars who were confronted with very specific legal questions and who were still sorting out both the answers to those questions and the methods of determining them. Al-Awza'i and his peers relied on a variety of means to determine correct answers to urgent questions and tried to be consistent, offering only occasional, rudimentary explanations of their reasoning. Clear paradigms for approaching legal methods remained elusive, both for al-Awza'i and for his contemporaries. The orderly approach of the surviving legal *madhhabs* was a product of later generations, not of the eponyms themselves.

Even though his students scattered and his *madhhab* never fully developed, al-Awza'i remained an important authority in Islamic legal discourse. It is remarkable that, despite lacking students and followers in later generations, al-Awza'i continued to be cited as a legal authority centuries after his death. His rivals and their followers still recognized him as someone worth citing and as someone whose legal judgments carried weight, despite the failure of his *madhhab*. His continued importance is underscored by the fact that later sources, perhaps with the exception of Abu Yusuf, did not merely use him as a straw man to refute or as a representative of now irrelevant Syrian practice. Instead, later sources cite him respectfully, treating him as a peer of the founders of the great legal *madhhabs* that survived and still thrive today.

Part of his continued prominence stems from the enmity Abu Yusuf held for him and from his objection to legal doctrines that eventually led to the radical reforms in taxation and land tenure during the early Abbasid period. Those who opposed these changes, whether for religious or financial reasons, could point to al-Awza'i as a counter-authority to the Hanafis advocating such changes. Curiously, neither his opponents nor his supporters made reference to al-Awza'i's association with the Umayyads. His extensive connections to the Umayyad caliphs will be discussed in more detail in chapter 5. The fact that al-Awza'i was able to escape the stigma of his attachment to the Umayyad regime and that his opponents did not simply dismiss his opinions as Umayyad views speaks to his stature as a scholar. Indeed, it almost seems as though, in the legal sources at least, his association with the Umayyads was erased to preserve his authority. The fact that a jurist associated with a failed and denigrated regime who had no followers a century after his death continued to be cited as a major legal authority is quite remarkable and underscores his importance for the development of Islamic law.

In conclusion, it may ultimately be impossible to reconstruct more than the broad outlines of al-Awza'i's jurisprudence, and even then conclusions must be tentative. From the material available, however, a general impression of his approach to jurisprudence can be posited. He was not slavishly devoted to any particular method of deriving legal rulings. When addressing details, he was at times lenient, at times stern, but always ultimately practical in his decisions. He commanded sufficient respect that he could state his conclusions without explaining himself. Most significantly, he continued to command the respect of later generations, despite producing no surviving tomes on jurisprudence and the collapse of his following not long after his death. In this sense, he seems to have been an anomaly, but an anomaly worthy of further attention.

AL-AWZAʿIʾS SCHOLARLY
MILIEU

Al-Awzaʿi was one of many religious scholars active during the late
Umayyad and early Abbasid period. While he was respected, influential, and well connected to the Umayyad authorities (as chapter 5
will explain more fully), others also vied for influence in the competitive but largely unstructured intellectual environment of the time.
Reconstructing the scholarly milieu of the late Umayyad and early
Abbasid period is challenging, in large part because scholarly networks
and hierarchies were amorphous and lacked any formal institutional-
ization, but also because important scholars' biographies were subject
to repeated revision by later generations to serve both hagiographic
and defamatory ends.

The *madrasa* system of formal schools sponsored by the government
or by wealthy individuals did not yet exist in al-Awzaʿiʾs time. There
was no specific place for scholars and their pupils to meet or study and
there was nothing resembling a standard curriculum. Mosques were
obviously convenient and appropriate venues for religious knowledge
seekers to gather. Some reports describe major mosques hosting multiple scholars' study circles simultaneously, with noted scholars claim-
ing corners or alcoves as their turf and students gathering around,
occasionally drifting from one circle to another seeking answers to
their queries, or perhaps merely following the crowd. In cities with
multiple mosques, individual mosques could come to be associated
with particular scholars and be frequented more exclusively by their
own students. Early examples of this phenomenon can be found in

the contentious garrison city of Kufa, discussed below. Private homes could also serve as fora for scholarly encounters, as could street corners, public squares, and even campsites. The lack of formal hierarchies meant that a scholar's prestige was, to some extent, simply a product of the number of students he attracted. In such an environment, fame could obviously be fleeting.

In the absence of academic institutions, it is also unclear how scholarly activity was funded. While scholars often embraced an ascetic lifestyle and many, though certainly not all, explicitly eschewed luxury, reports of involuntary poverty are exceptionally rare. Unfortunately, explanations for how religious scholars paid their bills are also rare. Many scholars, especially those interested primarily in *hadith* studies, worked as merchants as well. This profession was particularly suitable for sustaining scholarly endeavors because it facilitated travel over long distances, which was necessary for those gathering and circulating *hadith*. Biographies of some scholars mention (typically with little detail) their past military service, which would have entitled them to a pension. The amount of such payments and whether or not they provided sufficient support for a long and active scholarly life are not clear. Direct payments from students were frowned upon, though there are occasional reports of rulers or other elites offering scholars generous gifts to thank them for their assistance. Scholars apparently relied on a variety of means of support for their activities, and their income was likely sporadic, though seldom noted as being insufficient. There are no indications of any formal mechanisms to provide salaries to scholars, and their biographies seldom discuss their finances. Whether this was a taboo topic, or simply not considered to be relevant, is unclear as well.

During al-Awza'i's time, religious education operated under an informal mentorship system. Students pursuing religious knowledge sought out prestigious teachers from whom they absorbed as much as they could. However, the relationship between mentor and student was not exclusive. Instead, aspiring scholars benefited from working with multiple mentors as part of their training. The emerging focus on *hadith* transmission encouraged students to learn from as many teachers as possible in order to collect a larger corpus of material to pass on to their own students. Despite the pressure to pursue quantity, students still had to choose their teachers carefully. Transmitting *hadith* from a disreputable source might cast doubt on a student's judgment and possibly on the veracity of material he received from more respected scholars. In addition, as will be discussed in more detail below, students had to be aware of rivalries and conflicts between potential teachers. While overt factional divisions were rare among scholars at the time, studying with a known enemy would not endear a student to a potential teacher.

Modern scholarship has often proposed regional divisions in religious scholarship, suggesting that Islamic law and ritual practice were subject to local variations. The proposition that there were distinct Iraqi, Syrian, Medinan, and other legal traditions has some utility. It can explain the persistence of local customs and beliefs and acknowledges that the goal of legal and doctrinal uniformity, while perhaps laudable, is always elusive. The regional paradigm, however, has significant limitations. It presents a picture of local harmony among religious scholars while obscuring the rivalries between scholars within each region. The fact that early *ikhtilaf* works that document legal disagreements focus on individual scholars while seldom mentioning their geographical origins suggests that modern scholars have placed too much emphasis on regionalism. In addition, the emphasis on travel as a means to obtain knowledge in early Islamic society underscores the consensus that localized education was not sufficient. The realities of a highly mobile society also tended to dilute regional variations, as travelers, both scholars and non-scholars, spread their knowledge and experiences beyond their regions of origin. While it may have been easier to study in a provincial environment close to home, ambitious scholars had to pack their bags and broaden their horizons. Such travel may have been onerous, but it was quite common.

Despite pretensions to the contrary, the scholarly community of early Islam was not immune to politics. The historical and biographical sources offer a wide array of opinions about whether or not it was appropriate for scholars to associate with political authorities. Both modern and medieval sources have struggled to characterize the relationship between religious scholarship and worldly power. An opposition paradigm, according to which pious scholars were averse to political entanglements, has long dominated the discussion. However, biographies of individual scholars demonstrate that reality was more complicated. Some scholars were eager to serve political masters and achieved both prestige and financial success by doing so, while suffering little if any damage to their pious reputations. Others saw any interaction with government as a stain on one's integrity and shunned those who sullied themselves with such associations. To complicate matters further, some scholars were more nuanced in their choices and were willing to cooperate with some political leaders but not others. As chapter 5 will explain in more detail, al-Awza'i was willing to serve the Umayyads, but avoided entanglements with the Abbasids. Meanwhile, his Hanafi rivals served the latter, but condemned the former. For religious scholars, both aspiring and established, understanding the political leanings of potential teachers and colleagues was essential.

It is also important to remember that divisions between scholars extended to theological matters as well. Legal issues have attracted much more attention from both modern and medieval scholars because of their immediate practical implications. While contemplating questions about the nature of God was worthwhile, legal questions about inheritance, divorce, criminal offenses, and other matters could not wait. The urgency of legal disputes may in part explain why later madhhabs articulated legal differences more thoroughly than theological nuances. The literary production of later madhhabs, their lack of concern for theology, and their institutional dominance create the impression that legal divisions were far more important than theological differences, with the obvious exception of the eventual Sunni–Shi'ite divide, which was more political than religious in origin.

In al-Awza'i's time, the distinction between law and theology was less refined than it would eventually become. Scholars engaged in both "disciplines" and offered opinions about both. Some legal questions had theological implications and vice versa. Al-Awza'i's role in theological debates will be discussed in detail in the following chapter. For present purposes, it is important to acknowledge that theological differences could affect scholarly networks and mentoring relationships as much as legal or political disagreements did. Scholars whose legal credentials were flawless could find themselves shunned by some of their peers as a result of their theological views.

The scholarly environment in which al-Awzaʿi lived and worked was highly personal in nature. Students needed mentors and mentors needed students. They chose each other based on legal approaches, theological outlooks, and personal affinity. Ultimately, reputation mattered most. Those with good reputations attracted more students and could turn away students whom they disliked for personal or intellectual reasons. More reputable students could gain access to more esteemed mentors, enhancing the status of both. The result was an informal, ever-changing, amorphous hierarchy of scholars. Complicating matters further, scholars' reputations could improve or decline posthumously, as changes in consensus and distortions of historical memories took their toll.

In such an environment, rivalries between prominent scholars were complex, and sometimes subtle. Some rivalries were friendly, between scholars who had similar outlooks and mutual respect for one another. Other rivalries were more hostile. Divisions could stem from methodological disputes, political disagreements, old grudges, or perceived personal slights. Those who were friendly rivals might cooperate and learn from each other, while also sharing students. Their most successful students could eventually outshine them and become rivals as well. Hostile rivalries could be more volatile, and for historians more interesting. Students of some scholars did not mix with each other, and certainly did not study with their mentors' nemeses. Rivals might denigrate each other's abilities or piety, occasionally resorting to slander. In rare cases, those with political clout might use their connections to harm their foes financially or even physically.

The scholarly milieu in which al-Awzaʿi lived and worked was complicated, imprecise, and fraught with peril for both aspiring and established scholars. The fluidity of the environment, combined with the lack of venerable institutions, makes it difficult to reconstruct the scholarly landscape with much confidence. Compounding these difficulties is the reality that the reputations of individual scholars were subject to repeated revisions and realignments in the service of later agendas. In what follows, a number of rivals, friendly and otherwise, will be discussed. To begin, those who openly associated with al-Awza'i and were generally supportive of the Umayyad regime stand out as a distinct group of friendly rivals and collaborators. Al-Awza'i's Hanafi foes merit special attention on the hostile end of the spectrum. Finally, the case of the Malikis is somewhat peculiar and requires additional consideration.

PRO-UMAYYAD FRIENDS AND RIVALS

Al-Awza'i was hardly the first or the only religious scholar to cultivate a good relationship with the ruling Umayyad dynasty. From the dynasty's beginning, some religious scholars had worked closely with the Umayyads to advance their own visions of proper Islamic society, or out of a sense of duty to legitimate rulers. More cynically, perhaps a few simply followed the money the Umayyads could offer, as some later accusations suggest. These scholars included some of al-Awza'i's teachers, as well as a number of prominent contemporaries. The relationship between religious scholars and the Umayyads was complicated. It involved political choices and preferences, and both financial and other resources were at stake. Some scholars achieved glory or ignominy as a result of their coziness with political elites.

Sorting through the circumstances of scholars who were either obviously or purportedly associated with the Umayyad regime is also historiographically complicated. Changing attitudes toward particular rulers and government service in general are reflected in later biographies of scholars, creating at times contradictory images. Significantly, al-Awza'i and his contemporaries also lived through the Abbasid revolution, which brought with it an array of changing views about both the Umayyads and scholars' proper roles in society, as chapter 5 will explain more fully. Consequently, biographies of scholars show signs of revision and rehabilitation, sometimes in the service of contradictory, or perhaps just confused, agendas. Scholars' biographies and accounts describing the relationships between scholars should be read with this context in mind. Changing political agendas, as well as the aftermath of the Abbasid revolution, likely distorted the portrayal of scholarly networks, affecting the historical memory of their relationships with each other and with political authorities.

It is beyond the scope of this work to reconstruct in its entirety the scholarly network to which al-Awza'i belonged during the Umayyad period. This has already been done more thoroughly elsewhere. Instead, a brief discussion of a few prominent friendly rivals of al-Awza'i, who were also closely associated with the Umayyads in Damascus, will suffice to illustrate important aspects of the nature of the intellectual milieu in which he operated.

Al-Awza'i's predecessor Makhul al-Shami (d. *c.* 113/731) was arguably his generation's most prominent scholar in Damascus. He was also one of al-Awza'i's teachers, although their views on some matters diverged. In particular, Makhul was more tolerant than al-Awza'i was toward the Qadarites (discussed in more detail in chapter 4) who, contrary to Umayyad expectations, advocated for a doctrine of human free will. There is no indication of any confrontation or argument between the two over these issues. Nor is it clear whether their differences reflected their personal views, or were the consequence of a generational shift in attitudes toward certain religious dissenters. Whatever their differences over this heated theological issue may have been, they were not substantial enough to create a rift between them. In terms of legal methods, it is harder to distinguish between Makhul and al-Awza'i because so little of Makhul's jurisprudence survives.

It is curious that Makhul's death roughly coincided with al-Awza'i's emergence as an important legal adviser. Numerous reports indicate that al-Awza'i was first asked about legal issues in that year, when he was only twenty-five years old. While Makhul was alive, he would likely have been Damascenes' preferred source of legal advice. While no source explicitly suggests so, it is possible that al-Awza'i's youthful rise to prominence came as a result of his teacher's demise. Whether the young al-Awza'i was overshadowed by his teacher, or merely deferred to his predecessor's authority while Makhul was alive is also impossible to know. Regardless, none of Makhul's other students achieved al-Awza'i's status and influence, suggesting that he was, in some informal sense at least, Makhul's successor.

Al-Awza'i's most famous and influential colleague in Damascus was doubtless Ibn Shihab al-Zuhri (d. 124/742). While scholars have often associated al-Zuhri with Medina, he spent a considerable portion of his time in Damascus, where he was first employed by the Umayyad caliph 'Abd al-Malik (r. 65/685–86/705). During al-Awza'i's time, al-Zuhri served as a tutor to the caliph Hisham's sons, which would have made him a fixture at the caliphal court along with al-Awza'i. The two scholars shared predestinarian views, though al-Zuhri was less outspoken in his opposition to the Qadarites. Both were prominent and respected, but they appear to have carved out different niches in the scholarly world of Umayyad Damascus. Al-Zuhri was noted primarily for his copious *hadith* transmission, as well as his historical reports. While al-Awza'i was also a respected *muhaddith* who exchanged *hadith* with al-Zuhri and others, his legal acumen was the principal source of his stature. The two had different strengths to offer and appear to have performed complementary, albeit overlapping roles in Hisham's retinue. The two also differed in demeanor. As chapter 5 will discuss, al-Awza'i kept a relatively low profile and avoided openly engaging in political conflicts during his service to the Umayyads. Al-Zuhri, however, appears to have participated in, if not led, efforts to persuade Hisham to alter his succession arrangements and deny the caliphate to his nephew al-Walid b. Yazid. Al-Zuhri was controversial in other ways as well. He lived a sometimes flamboyant lifestyle and accumulated great wealth as a result of his service to the Umayyads. His penchant for luxury attracted criticism from both his contemporaries and later generations, sometimes coupled with suspicions that he had sacrificed his integrity in pursuit of the material comfort that his Umayyad masters could offer. Al-Awza'i's often austere lifestyle precluded such accusations of self-indulgence. While al-Awza'i and al-Zuhri were an oddly dissimilar pair competing for influence in the caliph's inner circle, there does not appear to have been any enmity or distrust between them. Their simultaneous presence in Hisham's service illustrates that scholars could assist the caliph in a variety of ways and that the scholarly community's hierarchies were not yet rigid enough to preclude peers from serving side by side.

Damascus remained a crucial arena for scholarly interactions and competition, but al-Awza'i's network of friendly rivals extended well beyond the capital. His closest colleague and most important collaborator was the Kufan-born Sufyan al-Thawri (d. 161/778). While Sufyan was seldom in Damascus, living instead in Kufa, Yemen, and other places, he and al-Awza'i both spent significant periods of time on the Byzantine frontier. They shared a number of students, the most important of whom was Abu Ishaq al-Fazari (d. c. 185/802). In his *Kitab al-siyar*, al-Fazari catalogues their views on the laws of war. The manner in which he presents the material suggests that he may have queried them about their views simultaneously, perhaps in joint audiences at the frontier.

There are also reports that al-Awza'i and Sufyan exchanged letters and books when they were away from the frontier. A number of accounts detail their encounters on pilgrimage, when they traveled and lodged together. These two scholars, who shared the same views on many legal and theological issues, appear to have chosen informal collaboration over rivalry, despite the competitive environment in which they worked. Their connections to each other are to some extent obscured in later sources. This is in part a product of choices they made after the Abbasid revolution. Al-Awza'i retreated to Beirut and continued to advise frontier fighters, while Sufyan spent most of his days in Yemen, gathering *hadith*. Later scholarly trends, which created different paradigms for classifying religious scholars, also contributed to their being recast as rivals rather than comrades.

While these are but a few of the many scholars with whom al-Awza'i had friendly but perhaps competitive relationships, their interactions illustrate important characteristics of the scholarly environment of the time. Scholars who had similar views on most issues could collaborate and share students. When these scholars disagreed, there is no evidence of enmity between them. Nor are there reports in which they criticize or insult each other in general. The contrasting lifestyles of al-Zuhri and al-Awza'i, along with their political disagreements, would certainly make stories of reproaches and arguments between them believable, yet no such reports exist. This suggests that, among this group, rules of decorum were followed and civility was expected. The absence of hostility between these prominent potential rivals facilitated their sharing of students as well as their simultaneous influence at the caliphal court. Other rivalries were less polite and created fault lines between scholars that could not easily be crossed.

THE HANAFIS: AL-AWZA'I'S FOES

Abu Hanifa (d. 150/767) is arguably the most famous and influential of al-Awza'i's scholarly contemporaries. He was the eponymous founder of the Hanafi legal *madhhab*, which has persisted until today. While Abu Hanifa himself did not advise or serve either the Umayyads or the Abbasids, his followers cultivated close relationships with the Abbasids, whom his disciple Abu Yusuf (d. 182/798) served as chief *qadi*. For several decades, Hanafis exercised tremendous influence over Abbasid legal and theological agendas. During the Umayyad period, however, Abu Hanifa and his followers were overshadowed by al-Awza'i and others and wielded little if any influence. Perhaps this explains, at least in part, their enmity toward al-Awza'i.

Despite the fact that al-Awza'i and Abu Hanifa were two of the most prominent scholars of their time, they do not appear to have met or interacted in any direct way. More surprisingly, Sufyan al-Thawri did not interact with Abu Hanifa either, despite the fact that they were both Kufans of the same generation. Scholarly divisions in Kufa were intense and long-standing. Sufyan's teacher al-Sha'bi (d. *c.* 100/718) openly feuded with Abu Hanifa's mentors over both substantive and superficial matters. The substantive issues upon which they disagreed were topics on which al-Awza'i and Sufyan agreed. Hence, it is not surprising that the Kufans' mutual enmity entangled al-Awza'i as well. As a general rule, students of the Hanafis did not mix with al-Awza'i and his associates and vice versa.

Al-Awza'i and the Hanafis clashed over important, substantive legal issues, specifically about aspects of the laws of war and taxation. Abu Yusuf wrote a refutation of al-Awza'i's views on these matters, purportedly in response to al-Awza'i's now lost critique of Abu Hanifa's interpretation. Somewhat ironically, Abu Yusuf's work, which has survived at least in part, is now a major source for uncovering al-Awza'i's legal opinions. Their disagreements about spoils of war and the status of captured land had obvious practical significance and political importance. The fact that al-Awza'i's Umayyad-era solutions were inconvenient for Abu Yusuf's Abbasid patrons only exacerbated the pre-existing division between the two scholarly factions.

Their division likely had methodological as well as practical roots. Abu Hanifa and his followers were closely associated with the deployment of human reason (ra'y) as a source of legal rulings. The nuances of their application of logical methods to legal and other questions are beyond the scope of this discussion. In general, they held that God is a logical being and that, consequently, God's creation and the rules his created beings are required to follow must be logical as well. For many, this presupposition opened the door to giving human logic preference over both divine revelation and earlier precedents. Al-Awza'i was not entirely opposed to the use of logical methods in religious thought. In both his legal rulings (discussed in the previous chapter) and his theological disputations (discussed in chapter 4) al-Awza'i did not hesitate to employ logical proofs in defense of his positions. However, his respect for precedence and revelation prevented him from veering as far toward logic as the Hanafis did. In al-Awza'i's time, the boundaries between methodologies were blurrier than they would eventually become. He and other non-Hanafis did not reject logical methods derived (directly or indirectly) from Greek tradition entirely, but they did not embrace such reasoning as firmly as Abu Hanifa and his disciples did. It is likely that the division between ra'y and hadith was less dramatic than later sources suggest and that this methodological dispute was not the root of the obvious antipathy between the Hanafis and al-Awza'i.

The rift between the two camps was real, however, and requires explanation. Personal slights and factional imperatives are not sufficient to account for such a deep and lasting divide. In all likelihood, the divide was as much theological as legal. The early Hanafis were often associated with the Mu'tazilites, who became the predominant theological force during the early Abbasid period. Seen as successors to the Qadarites, who will be discussed in more detail in chapter 4, the Mu'tazilites advocated for the doctrine of human free will as part of a broader embrace of human reason as a source of doctrine and law. Creeds ascribed to Abu Hanifa himself also point to his acceptance of the doctrine of human free will, although later documents of the Hanafi school offer a more nuanced approach to the problem of human volition. Al-Awza'i, by contrast, despised the Qadarites and others who questioned divine predestination, to the point of declaring that acceptance of human free will constituted apostasy. While there is no evidence of direct confrontations or epistolary debates between al-Awza'i and the Hanafis over theological issues, their differences over such a central doctrinal question surely contributed to the division between them. The severity of the enmity between al-Awza'i and Abu Hanifa, an animosity that apparently intensified between their respective followers, underscores the reality that theological disputes were as important as legal conflicts. The combination of disagreements about substantive legal issues, contrasting attitudes toward the Abbasids, and theological feuds created a divide that lasted for generations and that even the most ambitious and audacious of future students dared not attempt to cross.

THE MALIKIS

Malik b. Anas (d. 179/796), the eponymous founder of the Maliki legal *madhhab*, was also one of al-Awza'i's contemporaries. His rapport with Malik was both more complex and more amicable than his relationship with the Hanafis, such as it was. Malik was the leading legal thinker in Medina during his time. Unlike those of al-Awza'i, some of Malik's writings survive, likely due to the efforts of diligent students who were more successful in preserving their master's works than al-Awza'i's disciples were. As a jurist, Malik is typically associated with his hometown of Medina, where he spent most of his days, and is usually seen as a representative of a Medinan regional approach to law. Methodologically, he placed a great deal of emphasis on precedence and favored Medinan practice over that of other communities, based on the assumption that, as the home of the Prophet Muhammad, Medina was exemplary in its application of his message.

With the exception of his regional partiality for Medina, Malik's approach to legal reasoning did not differ greatly from al-Awza'i's. Both preferred precedence derived from the wisdom of the early community over unfettered human reasoning, setting them apart from the Hanafis. At the same time, neither entirely excluded the application of logic and analogy to legal questions. Malik appears to have relied more heavily on *hadith* citations than al-Awza'i did. However, this may be a product of later generations of Malik's followers' efforts to present his views in the increasingly prevalent *hadith* format, a transition that the demise of al-Awza'i's school precluded. The fact that Malik's most significant surviving work, the *Muwatta'*, is essentially a collection of *hadith* with commentary rather than a law book per se may have influenced later scholars to focus disproportionately on Malik's interest in *hadith* as well. While al-Awza'i and Malik approached legal questions with a similar method, their focus on precedence did not lead them to agree on every legal question. Instead, they sometimes preferred different precedents that supported opposite conclusions. In general, though, their disagreements on substantive law, while numerous, were not extreme enough to cause enmity between them or their followers.

Unlike al-Awza'i, Malik does not appear to have taken any strong theological stances. His voice is generally absent from the debate over human free will and predestination, the most contentious issue of his time. Malik also avoided political entanglements of any sort. There is no sign that he accepted employment from either the Umayyads or the Abbasids. Reports of his activities during the brief uprising led by Muhammad al-Nafs al-Zakiyya in Medina in 145/762 imply that he endorsed but did not participate in the rebellion. However, the fact that he suffered no repercussions from the Abbasids casts doubt on the accuracy of such accounts. While he kept a low political profile, he does not appear to have specifically condemned scholars who worked more closely with those in positions of power. Like many others, he counted more politically connected scholars such as al-Zuhri and al-Awza'i among his colleagues and teachers.

Malik's interactions with al-Awza'i are recounted in a number of sources. These typically describe meetings during pilgrimages to Mecca. In some accounts, Malik, Sufyan al-Thawri, and al-Awza'i appear to have been traveling and lodging together, suggesting that they shared a notable degree of mutual respect. Some of these reports include obvious hagiographic embellishments designed to clarify the relative merits of the three scholars. For example, Ibn 'Asakir includes a report that describes the three of them traveling en route to Mecca. Al-Awza'i is seated on a camel while Malik, on foot, holds the reins, and Sufyan walks ahead of them, leading the way. This and similar reports are clearly intended to imply a hierarchy among the three scholars, in which al-Awza'i generally occupies the top rank. While the stories may be exaggerated, they do illustrate the perception that the three scholars were on cordial terms and that there was no enmity between them. One cannot imagine anyone believing stories of similar interactions between al-Awza'i and Abu Hanifa or his students. Al-Awza'i's encounters with Malik were less frequent than his meetings with Sufyan. They shared fewer students and were not typically treated as close companions in the way that Sufyan and al-Awza'i were. Despite their competition for students and influence, however, they appear to have maintained a respectful relationship. This may explain, in part, the affinity later generations of al-Awza'i's followers had for the Malikis, although, conversely, reports of the two scholars' comradery may instead have been produced by those later generations to justify their own choices. The long-term importance of connections between Malik and al-Awza'i will be revisited in chapter 6.

This limited discussion of the scholarly environment of the late Umayyad and early Abbasid period is insufficient to capture all of the nuances of al-Awza'i's intellectual world, but offers at least a general impression of its complexities. In an environment that lacked established academic and religious institutions, lines between schools of thought were blurry at best. Competing scholars sometimes collaborated and shared students, and sometimes did not. Loyalties could be fleeting and relative, as students did not restrict themselves to a single mentor. In many instances, the distinction between student and teacher became fluid as well, with students transmitting *hadith* to their teachers, and established scholars exchanging knowledge with their peers.

While al-Awza'i's scholarly interactions were generally not contentious, two groups were clear exceptions whom he excluded from his intellectual circles. Abu Hanifa and his disciples did not mix with al-Awza'i and his followers. The sources are not littered with reports of either turning away students of the other. Nor are there stories of hostile personal exchanges between the two scholars. However, there are also no reports of the two or their students meeting and exchanging ideas or *hadith*, and there are occasional allusions to their deliberately avoiding each other. Their enmity is clear. Al-Awza'i also had no patience with Qadarites, who will be discussed in more detail in chapter 4. He openly condemned their beliefs and his only interactions with them were hostile. For example, after being forced to endure a long encounter with Thawr b. Yazid (d. *c.* 150/767), a noted Qadarite *hadith* transmitter, al-Awza'i is even reported to have written a specific refutation of his views, which has, of course, been lost. Obviously, no remotely perceptive Qadarite student would have ventured to seek knowledge from al-Awza'i. His hatred for the Qadarites is especially important to note in the context of a discussion of the scholarly milieu of the time because it is a reminder that divisions extended beyond legal disagreements and personal animosity and included a theological dimension as well.

An analysis of the scholarly environment of al-Awza'i's time is, unfortunately, complicated by later developments in the legal landscape and by the hagiographical tendencies inherent to biographies of important figures. It is important to acknowledge that later disputes between students of al-Awza'i and Abu Hanifa likely affected how the two of them were remembered in later historical sources, possibly amplifying their discord. The completeness of the rift between them in the sources and the lack of any contrary reports suggest, however, that their students' disputes had roots in their masters' time. The case of Malik is somewhat more complicated, as will be seen in chapter 6. The fact that many of al-Awza'i's followers in later generations eventually became Malikis may have encouraged them to soften differences between them and to emphasize their comradery instead. Although, the fact that most reports of their interactions imply al-Awza'i's superiority suggests that they predate his followers' turn toward Malik. The mere fact that such questions can be raised underscores the fluidity of the scholarly environment in which al-Awza'i operated. A world of personal relationships and flexible networks in which reputation mattered most can easily be affected by later historical revisions, subtle or otherwise.

AL-AWZA'I'S THEOLOGY

Al-Awza'i is not typically remembered as a major theological figure in early Islam. Discussions of early Islamic theology (*kalam*) often overlook him entirely, focusing instead on more famous thinkers, such as his predecessor al-Hasan al-Basri (d. 110/728), his contemporary Abu Hanifa, and later Iraqi Mu'tazilite thinkers. The importance of these early Iraqi thinkers may be exaggerated. To some extent, what distinguishes the more recognized early theologians is the simple fact that writings attributed to them have survived. Some of these, such as the "creeds" ascribed to Abu Hanifa, are rather slim works. Others, including al-Hasan's *Risala* (Letter), are more sophisticated, but are hardly comprehensive doctrinal statements. In a period from which few sources survive, those that are extant, even if their attribution is debated, attract scholars' attention.

By contrast, no written theological texts ascribed to al-Awza'i survive. While various sources note his writings, and even efforts by other scholars to refute him, the works themselves – whether creeds, treatises, or exegetical texts – are all lost. However, traces of his theological views are evident in other sources and display a notable degree of consistency while underscoring his importance as a theological thinker. Some of these traces are found in his legal opinions, while more are evident in anecdotes and *hadith* reports preserved primarily in biographical sources. Despite being underappreciated by modern scholarship, al-Awza'i's theological contributions are particularly important because of his close relationship with the ruling Umayyad dynasty, which could deploy its political power to impose doctrines it approved, and because of his residence in Damascus, which was the principal hub of intellectual, specifically theological, inquiry during the Umayyad period.

DAMASCUS AS A THEOLOGICAL CENTER

Modern scholarship has largely focused on Basra, Kufa, and Baghdad, rather than Damascus, as centers for the development of Islamic theology. However, during and even before the Umayyad period, Damascus and its Palestinian hinterlands were significant arenas for theological debate. This is largely due to the region's importance in Christian theological disputes during Byzantine times. When the Muslims took control of Damascus in 16/637, they found themselves ruling over a cosmopolitan, largely Christian population that included a scholarly class well versed in theological and other religious discourse. The denizens of ancient monasteries, both near the city and in more isolated locales closer to Jerusalem, had long traditions of contemplating, analyzing, and arguing about religious minutiae. In addition to Orthodox thinkers, a variety of other Christian sects and heterodox splinter groups were also present, creating a more complex, perhaps more contentious, intellectual milieu. The theological topics these Syrian Christians pondered touched upon issues with which their new Muslim rulers would also have to grapple. Their long engagement in such disputes facilitated the development of sophisticated approaches to argumentation, which their Muslim neighbors would quickly adapt to defend their beliefs against both Christian interlocutors and rivals within their own faith.

Despite its distance from Constantinople, Damascus remained closely engaged in doctrinal debates emanating from the imperial capital in pre-Islamic times. To a degree, Syrian scholars' physical separation from the capital and the watchful eyes of government authorities allowed them more independence in challenging or at least questioning doctrinal decrees from the Orthodox patriarch and/or the emperor himself. It is unclear whether the occasional dissent Syrian scholars displayed was a symptom of political dissatisfaction with Byzantine rule, or merely characteristic of the irascible nature of the scholarly community. Syrian Christian scholars were deeply engaged in the ongoing iconoclasm controversy, with many ultimately opposing Leo III's iconoclastic decree. They also delved into the complicated debates over Christology, the vexing, highly nuanced disagreements about how to explain the simultaneous humanity and divinity of Christ. Orthodox Syrian scholars, leaders of other sects, and assorted splinter groups offered a wide assortment of viewpoints on this issue. They also espoused a variety of positions on the question of human free will and predestination, an issue which Muslim scholars would have to address as well. These intra-Christian debates, or at least their written output, occurred predominantly in Greek, underscoring Syrian scholars' continued engagement with the larger Orthodox community even after the Arab conquests. However, at least a portion of these local Syrian Christians could likely communicate in Arabic as well. By the time al-Awza'i took up residence in Damascus, nearly a century after the initial Muslim conquest, surely a majority of the local Christians, particularly the educated elite, would have spoken Arabic. It seems highly unlikely that Christian leaders in the Umayyad imperial capital could have insulated themselves entirely from the imperial tongue.

Al-Awza'i and other Umayyad-era elites in Damascus would have had frequent contact with leaders of the Christian intellectual community, who continued to thrive and enjoy influence under Muslim rule. From the days of the initial conquest, Christian elites played a crucial role in Muslim Syria. The persistence of Greek as the primary language of administration until at least the reign of 'Abd al-Malik meant the retention of Greek-speaking Christians in bureaucratic positions. As was the case during the Byzantine period, these bureaucratic elites and the religious elites often came from the same prominent families. In some cases, important religious leaders served in bureaucratic roles for Muslim rulers, as they had under the previous Byzantine regime.

The most famous and important of these Greek-speaking Damascene elites was the family of Mansur b. Sargun, who according to some accounts negotiated the surrender of the city to the Muslims in 16/637. Mansur and his family continued to play important roles in the administration of the city, while maintaining their status as leaders in the Orthodox Christian community. Mansur's son appears to have been highly placed in the financial administration of the Umayyad Empire during 'Abd al-Malik's reign, and his grandson, the famous theologian John of Damascus (d. c. 132/749), succeeded his father in this role for later Umayyad rulers. The exact nature of their administrative positions is not clear, but they appear to have been near the apex of the Umayyad bureaucracy.

While Ibn Mansur and other members of the family were noted for their Christian piety, John stood out for his important contributions to Orthodox theology, and for his clashes with religious authorities from Constantinople. Both Greek and Latin theologians recognize John as the last of the early Church Fathers, underscoring the breadth of his influence. John of Damascus was also a fixture in the Umayyad administration, where he would have had regular contact with Muslim scholars. Details of his government service are elusive, though it is likely that he served in the upper echelons of the financial administration. His father reportedly managed the entire Umayyad fiscal bureaucracy, a position some suggest John inherited. Puzzlingly, scholars of Christian thought debate whether John knew Arabic at all. Given the positions that he held, his family background, and the ongoing Arabization of Damascus and Umayyad administration, it is implausible that he would not have had some degree of proficiency in Arabic. Despite the fact that John and al-Awza'i traveled in the same elite administrative circles, it is unlikely that the two actually met. John's withdrawal to monastic life in Palestine slightly precedes al-Awza'i's entry into elite circles in Damascus in 113/731. It is more likely that John met al-Awza'i's principal nemesis, Ghaylan al-Dimashqi, who in his position as director of the mint at Damascus during the reign of 'Umar b. 'Abd al-'Aziz (r. 99/717–101/720) surely would have met other highly placed financial officials like John and his father. Whether or not John influenced Ghaylan's views, particularly regarding human free will, is harder to gauge. While their views are similar, there is no convincing evidence of direct influence. However, it is worth noting that Ghaylan and his circle were often accused of teaching "Christian" doctrines.

John of Damascus is important for understanding al-Awza'i's theology because his views illustrate the theological environment in which

Muslim thinkers of al-Awza'i's era articulated their visions of Islam. John himself was aware of the conflicts among Muslim scholars at the time. His *Disputatio* implies that he engaged in theological debates with Muslim scholars, or at least offered guidance for those who did. He clearly had knowledge of the fault lines dividing Muslim thinkers. His well-documented views on human free will are particularly important, given that this was the focus of the most important Muslim theological dispute during al-Awza'i's time. Both medieval and modern scholars have argued that the doctrine of human free will, which was anathema to al-Awza'i and others, had Christian origins. However, it is difficult to find evidence of direct influence. John of Damascus does include basic guidance for arguing against predestination in his *Disputatio*, but his other writings on the topic are both more sophisticated and more insular. These works are infused with Aristotelian logic and references to earlier Christian texts. Their intended audience was clearly other Christian scholars within the Orthodox tradition. This suggests that debates between Christians and Muslims about predestination were peripheral for John and that he was focused instead on the more nuanced and mature Christian discourse.

While there are no clear signs of any direct influence John may have had on Muslim theological debates, his work remains important for understanding the intellectual environment in which al-Awza'i and his predecessors operated. It bears repeating that there is no evidence of direct encounters between al-Awza'i and John of Damascus or other Christian luminaries. Nor would John's writings, exclusively in Greek, have been easily accessible to al-Awza'i, even if he found them worth seeking out. His works are, however, indicative of the sophistication of the scholarly environment of Umayyad Damascus. It was a city with a long history as an intellectual center, with a particular focus on theology. The questions being debated there were relevant to both Christians and Muslims: the nature of God, sin and predestination, the propriety of icons and images. The arguments deployed were sophisticated, diverse, and infused with Aristotelian and other Greek logical influences.

It is also important to recognize that, despite eventually being eclipsed by other cities, during Umayyad times, Damascus was the

cultural and intellectual hub of the empire. Basra and Kufa were essentially military garrison towns that were diverse and complicated in
different ways, but lacked the scholarly sophistication and tradition of
Damascus. Baghdad, of course, did not yet exist. Later historical and
scholarly developments have distracted attention from Damascus, to
the detriment of our understanding of the development of Islamic law
and theology. It is in this scholarly milieu that al-Awza'i worked and
taught. It was an environment infused with theological questions and
memories of past scholarly disputes. It was a diverse community in
which Muslims and Christians, along with their ideas, mingled both
consciously and unconsciously. As a member of the Umayyad elite,
and a religious thinker, al-Awza'i could not have avoided encounters
with Christian intellectuals and their theories. Neither could he have
ignored theological questions altogether. His career reflects this environment, a mixture of dogmatic defense of his theological views and
acceptance of and respect for his Christian neighbors. Stories of his
advocacy for Christians (discussed in the following chapter) and of his
ecumenical funeral in Beirut underscore the complexity of his environment and his approach to it.

AL-AWZA'I'S THEOLOGICAL VIEWS

Al-Awza'i's views on theological questions and religious topics in
general are less well documented than those of his Christian contemporaries in Syria. Whatever theological writings he may have produced
do not survive. He left behind no treatises, no creeds, no lengthy
risalas, and no refutations of other scholars' views. Biographical and
other sources indicate that al-Awza'i committed his theological views
to writing, and that others saw the need to rebut his positions. One
report appearing in several sources indicates that the Abbasid caliph
al-Mansur (r. 136/754–158/775) asked his scribe Sulayman b. Mujalid
to write a refutation of al-Awza'i's views, but that the eminent official
demurred, admitting that he could not match al-Awza'i's brilliance.
Despite such attestations to al-Awza'i's importance, with the exception of Abu Yusuf's efforts to counter al-Awza'i's views on warfare

and spoils (discussed in chapter 2) neither his works nor their rebuttals survive. This is not especially unusual, given that the corpus of early Islamic theological texts is meager and that those that do survive are ascribed, correctly or otherwise, to scholars who enjoyed longer fame and more followers than al-Awza'i did. The contrast between this paucity of Muslim theological texts and the prodigious output of al-Awza'i's Christian contemporaries is curious and difficult to explain. John of Damascus and other Christian writers tapped into a centuries-long tradition of writing on theology and other religious topics. By contrast, Islam remained a relatively new faith. Early Muslims' focus on oral tradition and on maintaining at least the appearance of oral transmission may have contributed to the lack of texts as well. These contrasting paradigms for debating theology also illustrate that, while Damascus was certainly diverse and cosmopolitan, communities of religious scholars remained somewhat insular. Despite the lack of written texts from al-Awza'i, traces of his theological views can be found in biographical and other sources, which portray his opinions with surprising consistency.

One topic about which al-Awza'i opined was the definition of faith in Islam. Clarifying who was and was not a Muslim and outlining what conversion to the new faith required were important issues for the early Muslim community. The rights and privileges members of the Muslim community enjoyed differed from those of subject communities. Muslims and non-Muslims were treated differently in regard to taxation and a variety of legal matters. Rules regarding marriage, divorce, inheritance, legal testimony, punishment for crimes, and other aspects of life depended upon one's faith status. Tensions between encouraging conversion and guarding against false conversion (for the sake of tax reductions and other advantages) surfaced from time to time during the Umayyad period. In particular, 'Umar b. 'Abd al-'Aziz's decision to revise the tax code to benefit converts and the subsequent reversal of this policy produced a great deal of strife. For scholars, this was not merely a dispute about policy; it was also a religious question about the nature of conversion and about defining membership in the faith. Some, including those who would eventually be labeled as the Murji'a, took a lenient view, accepting anyone who professed to be a Muslim at his word. Others were more stringent, demanding that new converts' behavior reflect their professed faith, in some cases requiring rather onerous proof of their fidelity to Islam. Given al-Awza'i's prominence and position, it is not surprising that he expressed his opinion on this question.

The sources preserve at least three, not entirely consistent pieces of evidence concerning al-Awza'i's views on the definition of the faith. Abu Nu'aym offers a rare, direct statement of al-Awza'i's opinion on the matter. According to his report, al-Awza'i held that faith is not complete unless it includes profession (speech), deeds, and the intent to follow the *sunna*. Al-Awza'i added that those who profess their faith but do not know it in their hearts and demonstrate it through their deeds will not benefit and will ultimately be lost. Abu Nu'aym also reports a prophetic *hadith* transmitted on al-Awza'i's authority, in which the Prophet explains that faith has more than sixty facets, the most important of which is the profession of faith, and the least of which is the avoidance of harm. This prophetic statement also appears in several canonical *hadith* collections, but without al-Awza'i in its *isnad*. Instead, the report comes via other prominent, pro-Umayyad transmitters, suggesting that it represents a view accepted by the regime. The standard *hadith* collections do include one relevant report transmitted by al-Awza'i regarding the definition of the faith. In this saying, recorded in al-Bukhari's collection, Muhammad asserts that those who profess that there is only one God, that Muhammad is God's prophet, that Jesus is also a prophet, and that there is a heaven and a hell will be saved.

These three statements offer some insights into al-Awza'i's views regarding what is required for one to be considered a Muslim. All three clearly indicate that mere profession of the faith is not sufficient and that more is required. In this respect, they signal a rejection of the more inclusive Murji' view. At the same time, however, the statements are not entirely congruous. While al-Awza'i's own statement, and the first *hadith*, clearly demand more than a profession of faith, the second *hadith* focuses only on what one must profess. While the second *hadith* does not define additional requirements, its insistence on labeling Jesus as a prophet excludes Christians and Jews from the community, since Jesus was deemed divine by the former and a fraud by the latter. This may represent an effort to delineate clearly between Muslims and other monotheists. It is also important to note that al-Awza'i's own statement demands one's intent to follow the *sunna*, rather than success in actually doing so. This focus on intent is consistent with positions he espouses in legal contexts, where he holds that intentions matter more than actual deeds. These three statements do not offer a tidy summary of al-Awza'i's doctrine regarding the definition of faith, but they do exclude some positions while underscoring the complexity of the issue and the sophistication of al-Awza'i's approach to it.

Al-Awza'i's attitude toward proper behavior is perhaps best illustrated by reports about his own actions. He is typically remembered as an exemplar in terms of prayer, asceticism, and generosity. Reports of his own behavior contrast somewhat with his advice to others. He often appears to have held others to less rigorous standards than those to which he aspired for himself. This may reflect his preference for intention and effort rather than perfect results.

Biographical sources include numerous reports about al-Awza'i's prayers. One frequently repeated anecdote describes someone finding al-Awza'i's prayer mat saturated with sweat and tears from the intensity of his prayers. Many reports also note his habit of completing dozens more prostrations than were required in prayer. Others describe his supererogatory prayers extending through the night. He is also noted for the perfection of his technique while praying. His movements are described as smooth and flawless, as are his recitations. In regard to prayer, he is widely seen as an exemplar, both in his performance of his prayers and in their intensity and frequency. His authority regarding proper prayer is also evident in the legal literature, where he is cited frequently. In fact, his legal responses to questions about prayer far outnumber those regarding warfare, a topic on which he is remembered as a pre-eminent expert.

Al-Awza'i's discussion of prayer illustrates the same nuance noted above regarding his attitude toward the *sunna* in general. On the one hand, reports from al-Awza'i about prayer offer painstaking, meticulous detail about how to perform certain aspects of prayer. He clearly

believes that there is a correct way, and an incorrect way, to perform one's daily prayer duties. On the other hand, many of his legal
responses regarding prayer are less stringent. There is no condemnation for those who forget words, motions, or even entire prayers.
He allows accommodation for those who arrive late, or who fail to
perform proper ablutions. He is pragmatic in dealing with mistakes
made by the *imam* while leading prayers. Underlying his simultaneous
meticulousness and leniency is the concept of intention. As in other
aspects of the faith, there is a proper way to do things, but none will
reach perfection. What matters to al-Awza'i is simply that the faithful
intend to act properly and put forth their best effort.

The role of asceticism in early Islam, and particularly among prominent early Muslim scholars, is somewhat complicated. The later Sufi
movements that would eventually combine mysticism with asceticism and come to define both had not yet developed in al-Awza'i's
time, although the movements' precursors are occasionally evident.
As the Sufi trend emerged and grew, its advocates tended to claim
early Muslim thinkers as their own. It may not be an exaggeration to
suggest that every early Muslim luminary who ever prayed an extra
prayer or fasted an extra day was at some point claimed as a proto-Sufi
of some sort. The most prominent example of this tendency was al-
Awza'i's predecessor al-Hasan al-Basri who, in all likelihood, was a
pious, ascetic scholar, but who was transformed by some later traditions into one of the original Muslim mystics. Sorting truth from later
fiction is particularly difficult in regard to asceticism and mysticism.

Like al-Hasan, al-Awza'i attracted a certain degree of exaggeration about his asceticism. Dreams are a common vehicle for mystical
insights in biographies of the pious. In one of the few surviving stories of al-Awza'i's own dreams, Abu Nu'aym reports that al-Awza'i
described being lifted into the sky, where angels quizzed him about
al-'amr bi-l-ma'ruf, the expectation that Muslims implore people to
do good while condemning bad behavior. Al-Awza'i simply told the
angels that they knew better than he did, prompting them to lower
him back to earth without further inquiry. In another of his dreams, the
angels bemoan creation without explaining why. These dreams offer
little about al-Awza'i or his attitudes toward mystical enlightenment,

though perhaps the first underscores his modesty. More frequent reports involve others dreaming about al-Awza'i. These dreams typically emphasize modesty, piety, and the need to prepare for judgment day. There are also examples of other scholars' dreams alerting them to al-Awza'i's death. In all likelihood, these dreams are later inventions that add a mystical element to al-Awza'i's more mundane asceticism.

Many reports emphasize other aspects of al-Awza'i's asceticism. Several assert that al-Awza'i was never seen laughing. He even told one of his followers not to laugh or smile, lest others emulate him in such frivolity. Some report that he never cried either, though this seems to contradict stories of his tear-soaked prayer mat. Al-Awza'i also regularly emphasized the virtue of silence, telling his followers that they should contemplate death and focus on works rather than words. He was reportedly obsessed with judgment day and with death, and focused on being prepared for either. This detached, stoic demeanor is, of course, commonly ascribed to mystics and ascetics. It is difficult to ascertain whether these reports accurately represent al-Awza'i or whether they are merely overused tropes applied to holy men in both Islamic and pre-Islamic contexts. In any case, his piety, self-denial, and prayers seemed to attract more notice than did his contemporaries' similar qualities.

Reports of al-Awza'i's generosity and disdain for material wealth also present some difficulty. A number of sources indicate that he was entered in the *diwan* to receive a stipend at a young age, after unspecified military or other government service. By contrast, other sources claim that he refused any sort of stipend. There are a number of reports in which al-Awza'i gives more alms than required. In some anecdotes, those who seek his advice give him usually modest gifts, which he then passes on to the poor. In one anecdote he warns his son that it is inappropriate to appear to be excited when people offer gifts. In other instances, he refuses gifts or payment for his assistance. These stories and others illustrate the general disdain for and indifference toward material wealth that one might expect from an ascetic concerned only with death and judgment day.

However, other anecdotes suggest that al-Awza'i had considerable resources at his disposal. For instance, in one story, a local Christian in Beirut sought al-Awza'i's help in resolving a tax dispute. When his appeal to the *kharaj* tax administrator failed, al-Awza'i gave the Christian the 80 *dinars* he thought he was owed, and even tried to return the jar of honey the Christian had given him to thank him for his efforts. Accounts of al-Awza'i's death also belie any suggestion of self-imposed poverty. According to most reports, al-Awza'i was found dead in the bath at his house (facing Mecca, of course). He had been locked in the bathhouse accidentally, either by his wife or his servant. While these stories may be embellished in various ways, they do indicate that al-Awza'i had a house with its own bath, a rather luxurious amenity for the time, as well as a servant to tend him. His home, and subsequently his tomb, were located in a part of Beirut that had been especially prosperous during Byzantine times, as evidenced by the remains of opulent villas from the late fourth or early fifth century CE. Even if the neighborhood had lost some of its prosperity by al-Awza'i's time, the description of his house with a bath suggests that it was hardly a destitute part of the city. Al-Awza'i also had sufficient money at hand to provide sizable donations to those whom he perceived to have been wronged. While al-Awza'i may have been modest and frugal, he was certainly not a pauper. The sources do not clearly indicate from whence al-Awza'i's wealth derived. Perhaps he actually did accept stipends, or perhaps he did not reject every gift he was offered. It is clear, though, that he had access to considerable resources. The historical and biographical sources do not address the paradox of his simultaneous wealth and asceticism, suggesting perhaps that such contradictions were not considered unusual or important.

Overall, al-Awza'i appears to have been a pious, moderately ascetic man. He deprived himself to some extent, but retained possessions and even a taste for certain luxuries. He prayed more than others, but did not retreat to become a hermit immersed in constant prayer. He encouraged others to be modest and humble, but does not appear to have condemned those who were not. His attitudes and behavior were likely not particularly unusual when compared to other devout Muslims in the community. What stands out is the extent to which he was praised for relatively moderate deeds. This is likely a product of his fame rather than his unusual piety.

AL-AWZA'I AND THE QADARITES

While al-Awza'i appeared to be somewhat moderate in his religious views on many topics, the opposite was true in regard to the question of human free will. He was famously uncompromising in his condemnation of those who denied predestination. His vigorous stance, combined with the importance of this issue in early Islam, make this the doctrinal position for which al-Awza'i is best known. The issue of human free will is a conundrum in any monotheistic context. Reconciling belief in an omnipotent, omnipresent, benevolent god with the reality of evil and sin in the world is not a simple intellectual endeavor. For centuries prior to Islam, monotheists of all types had confronted the issue with varying success. As discussed above, free will was a major topic of debate for John of Damascus and other theological minds in Syria and elsewhere when the Muslims arrived on the scene. Given that Syrian Christians were both potential converts and useful employees for the Umayyads, it is inevitable that Muslim thinkers would have to confront the issue of predestination in their own faith.

The debate over free will also had important political implications for the Umayyads. Their conception of the office of caliph combined temporal and religious authority. Hence, they could not simply ignore doctrinal questions. With rare exceptions, the Umayyads embraced and promoted the doctrine of predestination. They claimed that God had destined them to rule and that their actions were God's will. Consequently, resistance to their rule was futile because God had appointed them. Curiously, there does not seem to be any evidence of challengers arguing that their opposition was also divinely willed. Most Umayyad rulers appealed to predestination sparingly, relying instead on the grandeur of the office, the support of the religious establishment, and sometimes raw power to maintain their positions. Others deployed predestination more daringly. Al-Walid b. Yazid (r. 124/743–125/744) stretched the doctrine to its extreme, arguing that all of his actions were willed by God and that he was, therefore, unaccountable for any of his deeds, no matter how debaucherous or vindictive. Others were less willing to accept sinful acts and unjust rulers as God's will. They expected rulers, and humans generally, to be held accountable for their good and evil actions. These dissenters came to be known as the Qadarites, either because they denied God's determinative power (*qadar*), or because they asserted that humans had such power. The debate over human free will and its political implications likely date from very early in the Islamic period, in part because of its inherent importance and in part because of its prevalence in territories Muslims conquered. The debate was apparently proceeding in earnest by the time of 'Umar b. 'Abd al-'Aziz, when the caliph himself purportedly engaged in such discussions and prominent scholars such as al-Hasan al-Basri were interrogated about their views.

Al-Awza'i played a crucial role in the debate during the reign of Hisham. He also appears as an important source of information about proponents of human free will in earlier times. He asserted that none of the Prophet Muhammad's companions denied predestination. This places the origins of Qadarite doctrine well after the death of the Prophet, making it an innovation (*bid'a*) that was contrary to the beliefs of the early community. Al-Awza'i specifically traces the birth of the Qadarite movement to Ma'bad al-Juhani (d. *c.* 80/699). Ma'bad was widely labeled as the first to teach "lies about *qadar*." He was a prominent scholar who even served as a tutor for one of 'Abd al-Malik's sons before going doctrinally astray. Al-Awza'i attributes Ma'bad's fall to the allure of Christian teachings, which he learned from an apostate teacher. The attribution of Qadarite doctrine to Christian origins is rhetorically important, since it labels Qadarite views as outside the faith. Such an attestation is, however, also quite plausible. As discussed above, the Orthodox Christians of Syria, including John of Damascus, openly espoused such views and attacked Muslim predestinarian doctrine. It is possible that Ma'bad encountered such thoughts through Christian interlocutors, or that the question of human free will was simply in the air in Damascus during his time. It is interesting that al-Awza'i, who never met Ma'bad, remained the principal source for labeling him as a Qadarite. Whether this reflects al-Awza'i's interest and knowledge about the subject, or whether he had other motives for the attestations, such as distancing the doctrines from the Prophet's companions, is not clear.

In his own time, al-Awza'i had a number of encounters with leading Qadarites of his day, none of which was pleasant. There are a number of reports in which al-Awza'i debates and rebuts unnamed Qadarites as well as more famous thinkers, such as the *muhaddith* Thawr b. Yazid (d. *c.* 150/767). Al-Awza'i was always said to have given questions about *qadar* careful consideration before answering. However, he never deviated from condemning the Qadarites. Many hurled insults at the Qadarites and attached derogatory labels to them. Al-Awza'i went further, though, deeming the Qadarites to be *kafir*s, or apostates. For him, they were not merely guilty of heresy or ignorance, they had abandoned the faith altogether. Consequently, they deserved death.

The most famous and influential of al-Awza'i's Qadarite opponents was Ghaylan al-Dimashqi, about whom a fair amount has been written elsewhere. Like his alleged teacher Ma'bad al-Juhani, Ghaylan enjoyed access to the caliph's inner circle and held prestigious positions. The pinnacle of his administrative success came during the reign of 'Umar b. 'Abd al-'Aziz, when he served as the director of the mint in Damascus. His appointment to this position was important for several reasons. First, it was a job that required particular expertise, suggesting that Ghaylan had long-term experience in the mint, possibly even dating back to the days of 'Abd al-Malik's dramatic coinage reforms. Second, as part of the empire's monetary administration, he likely would have met other high-ranking financial officials, such as John of Damascus and his family, who may have exposed him to "Christian" Qadarite doctrines. Finally, the question of whether or not he espoused Qadarite views while in 'Umar's employment or adopted them later is still the subject of some debate. 'Umar was famously tolerant toward unorthodox views. Whether or not that tolerance extended to the Qadarites is still contested.

By the time al-Awza'i encountered Ghaylan, he was no longer in government service and no longer enjoyed the caliph's good graces. Instead, he had become a major leader of the Qadarite movement, whose size and influence are difficult to gauge. Unlike earlier Qadarite thinkers, Ghaylan is reported to have written many letters and treatises about his views, none of which survive and none of which became specific focal points in his later interrogations. During the reign of

Hisham, Ghaylan and his movement had grown large enough to be seen as a political as well as a doctrinal threat. Consequently, Ghaylan and his followers had to be condemned more forcefully.

There are a number of accounts of Ghaylan's trial and execution in which a variety of noted scholars play central roles. The accounts in which al-Awza'i prosecutes Ghaylan are the most likely to be authentic, for reasons explained elsewhere. These accounts are important at present not because of what they offer about Ghaylan and the Qadarites, but because of what they reveal about al-Awza'i's stature, views, and argumentation. In all of the accounts, al-Awza'i acts as prosecutor on Hisham's behalf and in his presence. Al-Awza'i begins by establishing the ground rules for their exchange, asking Ghaylan how many questions he would agree to answer. They ultimately settle on three questions. This formality suggests that the two participants were familiar with the rules of engagement for theological debates and that such interrogations were a common occurrence. The questions al-Awza'i asks are binary, and in each case Ghaylan cannot respond positively or negatively. Instead, he laments the difficulty of the questions and refrains from answering. The questions themselves appear to be quite general, but mask complex theological arguments. Al-Awza'i first asks whether God can ordain what he forbids, then he asks if God can allow something he did not ordain, and finally he asks whether God can command that which he also forbade. The abstract questions and Ghaylan's silence apparently confused the caliph who, after condemning Ghaylan to death, asks al-Awza'i to explain his queries. Al-Awza'i then reveals what the questions are actually about. The first question, about God ordaining what he forbids, relates to Adam's consumption of the forbidden fruit. The second question, about whether God could permit something he did not command, refers to Satan's refusal to bow before Adam. The final question, about God commanding what he forbids, concerns the prohibition on eating pork, the consumption of which God commands in times of desperate necessity. Al-Awza'i then cites a number of Qur'anic verses that are interpreted as a rejection of human free will.

These stories of Ghaylan's condemnation have a dramatic flair and may have been embellished for hagiographic or entertainment purposes.

However, they also offer important evidence of both the intellectual environment in which al-Awza'i worked and the theological views he and his Umayyad patrons espoused. The debate did not consist of the two opponents flinging Qur'an and *hadith* citations at each other to support their positions and confirm their knowledge of religious texts. Instead, it is a logical duel, grounded in binary argumentative tactics. In one account of the postlude to the debate, Hisham asks al-Awza'i what he would have done if Ghaylan had answered in particular ways. Al-Awza'i then explains the logical trap he had set for Ghaylan, allowing him no escape regardless of his response. Ghaylan obviously foresaw al-Awza'i's next steps, like a chess player who knows he has lost several moves before the inevitable checkmate. This exchange and its explanation underscore the sophistication of theological arguments in Umayyad Damascus. Here again, the echoes of Christian theological disputes are evident. In fact, two of the three examples al-Awza'i cites in his explanation to the caliph could easily have been deployed in Christian debates about the same topics. While the Muslims may have been relative newcomers to the dialectical theological games played in Damascus, by al-Awza'i's time, they clearly knew (and accepted) the rules, which were steeped in Greek logic more than in scripture.

The stories of Ghaylan's prosecution and execution also demonstrate the extent of Umayyad rulers' commitment to the doctrine of predestination, their determination to expunge the Qadarite heresy, and al-Awza'i's role in this effort. Al-Awza'i is universally described as a fierce foe of the Qadarites and a staunch advocate for predestination. During his time in Damascus, the Umayyad regime became increasingly intolerant toward the Qadarites. Whether or not al-Awza'i was partially responsible for this heightened persecution of the Qadarites is harder to determine. However, his doctrinal views on the matter are quite clear, as is his participation in efforts to impose predestinarian orthodoxy.

CONCLUSIONS: AL-AWZA'I'S THEOLOGY

While available sources allow a partial understanding of al-Awza'i's views on a variety of theological issues, they do not permit a complete

reconstruction of his religious doctrines. Material directly attributable to al-Awza'i is rather scarce. Any creeds or treatises he may have
written do not survive and are not quoted in other sources. Nor are
lengthy refutations of his views extant, assuming those alluded to in
later sources ever existed. This is not unusual for the period. Written
evidence of theological disputes and the views of those engaged
in them is almost nonexistent for the Umayyad period. Given that
al-Awza'i was remembered primarily as a legal scholar rather than as
a theologian and that his disciples were unsuccessful in maintaining a
sustained al-Awza'i "school," it is not surprising that his theological
works have not been preserved.

Despite this, traces of his theological views can be found scattered
in a variety of sources. He clearly engaged in debates about the nature
of faith and the nature of God. His views on these topics are not as
precise as one might wish, but distinguish themselves from the Murji'a
and other groups. He is also remembered for his contributions to ritual
and devotional realms. In these regards, he held himself to painstaking
standards, but was more lenient with others, focusing on intention
more than on actions themselves. In many aspects of piety, he could
be regarded as something of a moderate, praying more than one is
expected to but not becoming a hermit, showing indifference toward
wealth and ease but not embracing self-imposed poverty, living as an
ascetic, but not a mystic.

Only in regard to human free will was al-Awza'i entirely uncompromising. He saw Qadarite doctrines as a threat to the faith and
deemed those who preached such views to be apostates who must be
purged. There was no room for nuance or tolerance on this issue.
Al-Awza'i played a pivotal role in the debate over predestination and
human free will. The significance of his prosecution of Ghaylan cannot be understated. Ghaylan was both the most popular leader of the
Qadarites and, by most reports, their most prolific thinker. The fact
that Hisham turned to al-Awza'i for his interrogation speaks to his perceived expertise on the topic. The arguments presented in accounts
of their exchange also illustrate that, despite the lack of written treatises, al-Awza'i and his contemporaries engaged in complex debates,
infused with logical tools adopted from the Greek Aristotelian

tradition. The exchange also underscores the extent to which Muslim theological debates paralleled debates within the Christian community in both substance and technique. While one cannot confidently assert Christian influence over the development of Muslim theology, it is clear that the theological and intellectual environment of pre-Islamic Damascus was consequential and affected both the topics discussed and the manner in which those discussions occurred.

While the study of Islamic theology often focuses on Iraqi scholars from later times, it is important to recognize that Damascus was the first milieu in which sophisticated debates about Islamic theology occurred. In the late Umayyad period, al-Awza'i was arguably the most prominent theological thinker in Damascus and was at the center of the most contentious religious disputes of his time. Despite the fragmentary record of his contributions, they must be recognized and appreciated for their influence on later Islamic thought and the approach to debating about it.

5

AL-AWZA'I AND THE
POLITICAL ELITE

In most modern scholarship, al-Awza'i is depicted as showing disdain, if not outright hostility toward political entanglements of any sort. In later imaginations, both medieval and modern, scholars of al-Awza'i's era avoided associations with the ruling elites. Within a century of al-Awza'i's death, the prevailing view was that politics and piety were incompatible and that fraternizing with cold, calculating, frequently immoral rulers was to be avoided at all costs. Modern scholars have largely adopted these medieval judgments uncritically, portraying the pious scholars as opponents, either quiet or vocal, to tyrannical caliphs whose commitment to the religion was at times dubious. To a great extent, this portrayal is an overgeneralization, based on sources and narratives crafted in response to religio-political disputes during the Abbasid period. Umayyad-era religious scholars, who worked in a different religious and political environment, were swept up into this narrative of resistance, often despite evidence to the contrary.

These medieval scholarly trends and their modern extensions affected al-Awza'i's image as well. The biographical and historical sources offer some fodder for remembering al-Awza'i as a political rejectionist. There are reports of his refusal to accept specific government positions or stipends from government officials. There are also dramatic stories of al-Awza'i's hostile encounters with Abbasid officials in the aftermath of their victory in 132/750. However, a closer examination of al-Awza'i's interactions with various government officials demonstrates that it is far too simplistic to assert that he had a general aversion to politics. While numerous stories of his initial interactions with Abbasid officials portray his resistance to their authority in various ways, other reports suggest that he had a more complicated and less hostile relationship with the new regime. By contrast, there is no indication whatsoever of antipathy between al-Awza'i and the Umayyads. Instead, as will be discussed below, he willingly served Umayyad leaders and advised them on important doctrinal and legal matters. The aversion to government service ascribed to him by later scholars would be better characterized as a rejection of the Abbasid revolution. Al-Awza'i's views on the proper relationship between scholars and leaders were complex and reflected his understanding of political legitimacy as well as the role of pious thinkers in Islamic society.

AL-AWZA'I AND THE UMAYYADS

Al-Awza'i had the good fortune to reside in Damascus when the Umayyad Empire was at its peak, during the long reign of Hisham b. 'Abd al-Malik. He settled there around 113/731, at the age of twenty-five, after spending several years traveling and studying. Al-Awza'i quickly established his reputation as a jurist and, despite his relative youth, became a leading figure in the circle of religious scholars in Damascus. At some point, his legal acumen attracted the attention of the caliph himself, and he became part of Hisham's inner circle. The exact nature of his relationship with his Umayyad patrons is elusive. His role in the prosecution of Ghaylan al-Dimashqi, discussed in the previous chapter, demonstrates his importance and reputation, as well as his availability and willingness to serve the caliph. Other reports suggest that al-Awza'i read at least some caliphal correspondence and imply that he assisted Hisham in formulating his replies. There is no indication, however, that al-Awza'i formally served as a scribe for the caliph. Nor does any source assign a specific title to al-Awza'i's position, or indicate what remuneration, if any, he received for his services. Reports of his interactions with the caliph and other elites suggest that he was part of the caliph's inner circle and served in a discreet advisory capacity. There is no sign that he sought honors, official positions, or financial rewards for his service. There are also no indications that he had any aversion to serving Hisham or that he sought to evade such duties.

A number of al-Awza'i's statements, reported in various sources, underscore his acceptance of Umayyad authority and legitimacy. While some of these are a bit oblique, they consistently illustrate his loyalty to the Umayyads while also explaining his initial rejection of Abbasid legitimacy. The most famous of his assertions of Umayyad legitimacy were his claims that the correct practice of the community continued until the murder of al-Walid b. Yazid in 126/744. As discussed in chapter 2, al-Awza'i held that the continuous practice of the Islamic community which some modern scholars label as "living tradition" was normative, even after the death of the Prophet Muhammad and his immediate companions. For al-Awza'i, sustained community practice was not mere custom, but rather a manifestation of God's guidance. Al-Awza'i was not alone in extending the ranks of exemplars whose actions were part of the *sunna* beyond Muhammad. Many scholars considered the first four caliphs to be sources of religious guidance, even labeling them as the Rashidun, or rightly guided ones. Scholars occasionally added 'Umar b. 'Abd al-'Aziz to their lists of exemplars as well. Al-Awza'i, however, expanded the ranks of the rightly guided further than other scholars did.

According to al-Awza'i's view, all of the Umayyad caliphs, at least until al-Walid's murder, could serve as exemplars and, more importantly, as sources of legal authority. Unfortunately, al-Awza'i did not explicitly articulate this view or explain its intricacies and potential contradictions, at least not in any extant source. One could cynically argue that al-Awza'i's advocacy for caliphal religious and legal authority derived from his close relationship with Hisham, a caliph who conveniently listened to al-Awza'i's counsel. However, with few exceptions, the earlier Umayyad caliphs were consistent in their doctrinal views, particularly in regard to issues such as *qadar*, about which al-Awza'i had particularly strong views. The single doctrinal exception might be 'Umar b. 'Abd al-'Aziz, but even he did not stray far from traditional Umayyad views.

Al-Awza'i's interactions with Hisham illustrate the peculiarity and complexity of his position. On the one hand, al-Awza'i sees the caliph as a source of religious authority. On the other hand, reports of his interactions with his caliphal patron describe the caliph seeking advice from scholars rather than simply dictating doctrine. Some of the anecdotes discussed in the previous chapter portray the caliph's apparent ignorance of the scriptural foundations and arguments supporting particular doctrines he espouses. The caliph appears simultaneously as a religious authority and as someone lacking theological brilliance. Perhaps his willingness to seek scholarly counsel from the right scholars is what made him an exemplar in al-Awza'i's eyes. It is also important to note in this regard the contrast between the caliphs' role as religious exemplars and their morally dubious personal conduct. As a member of Hisham's inner circle, al-Awza'i could not have been unaware of the debauchery of the Umayyad family. While Hisham was by most accounts stern, pious, and cautious, his sons were not. Nor were some previous caliphs who, despite their best efforts, failed to conceal their moral indiscretions entirely. Hisham's successor, al-Walid, whom al-Awza'i implicitly accepts as the last of the rightly guided caliphs, was famous for flouting every norm and flaunting his bad behavior. Al-Awza'i cannot have been unaware of al-Walid's antics, yet he did not condemn his actions. The contrast between al-Awza'i's personal piety and his apparent acceptance of immoral caliphs as religious exemplars cannot easily be explained. Other reports suggest that he believed that loyalty to the caliph was required, regardless of his actions. This viewpoint is consistent with al-Awza'i's strict predestinarian doctrine and with the caliphal absolutism he tended to favor.

One of the reports that help to explicate the apparent contradictions in al-Awza'i's views is an obscure *hadith* transmitted on his authority and included in Ibn Maja's *hadith* collection, despite some commentators' doubts about its veracity. In this *hadith*, the Prophet Muhammad asserts that the Israelites remained just until the children of foreign slave women rose up among them and led them astray. The biblical reference is uncertain and on its surface this *hadith* is not inherently political. Closer scrutiny reveals that this report has significant political connotations for al-Awza'i's time and reflects his views on political legitimacy. In an Umayyad context, the report could represent simple Arab chauvinism and contempt for the *mawali*, the predominantly non-Arab converts and their descendants. However, al-Awza'i did not otherwise disparage non-Arabs or display any sort of Arab pride. Instead, the reference to children of foreign slaves is much more specific. The first Umayyad ruler born to a slave mother was Yazid b. al-Walid (r. 126/744), who was responsible for the murder of al-Walid b. Yazid. While his mother was a concubine, she was also a descendant of the Sassanian royal family. Yazid famously took pride in his maternal ancestry, perhaps emphasizing her lineage to distract from her servile status. Not only was Yazid the child of a foreign slave woman, he was also an avowed Qadarite. From al-Awza'i's perspective, this certainly qualified Yazid as one who led the people astray. The *hadith* complements al-Awza'i's position that the murder of al-Walid marked the end of the era of just community practice. Moreover, it places al-Walid's fall in a broader context of salvation history by creating parallels to biblical disasters and by demonstrating that the Prophet Muhammad predicted this turn of events, implying that the fall of the dynasty at the hands of the heretical son of a foreign slave woman had been predestined, undermining the Qadarite narrative of these events.

This obscure *hadith* can also be understood as a reference to the subsequent Abbasid revolution. The first Abbasid ruler, Abu al-'Abbas al-Saffah (r. 132/750–136/754), was the son of a Berber slave woman. His successor, Abu Ja'far al-Mansur (r. 136/754–158/775), was also the son of a slave woman. In addition, the last Umayyad caliphs, Ibrahim b. al-Walid (r. 126/744) and Marwan b. Muhammad (r. 126/744–132/750), both of whom failed to reunite the empire, were also born to slave mothers. Hence, after the murder of al-Walid, every caliph or purported caliph during the remainder of al-Awza'i's life could fall into the category Muhammad warned about in this cryptic *hadith*. Curiously, al-Mansur's successor, al-Mahdi (r. 158/775–169/785), whose more cordial relationship with al-Awza'i will be touched upon shortly, was the first Abbasid ruler to be born to a free mother of noble Arab lineage. Whether or not al-Awza'i's attitude toward the Abbasids might have changed had he lived long enough to see al-Mahdi's rise to power can only be left to speculation.

While this *hadith* report about the failures of the ancient Israelites is obscure and often overlooked, it is important for evaluating al-Awza'i's understanding of both the Umayyads and their Abbasid usurpers. It provides a genealogical justification for the rejection of every caliph who followed al-Walid, whose demise marked a turning point in al-Awza'i's opinion. It also undermines the Qadarite justification for rebellion, namely the demand that rulers be held personally accountable for their evil actions. Al-Walid fell not because of his moral choices, or those of his opponents. Instead, the confluence of heresy and genealogy that produced rebellion and then revolution was predicted by the Prophet Muhammad and foreordained by God. Consequently, the revolutionaries lose their luster and the Qadarites are reduced to being cogs in the divinely dictated machinery of salvation history. For someone holding al-Awza'i's views, this *hadith* report is obviously quite useful.

Al-Awza'i also transmitted a version of a more common *hadith* that helps to explain his objection to the Qadarite seizure of power and the subsequent Abbasid revolt along with his relatively passive response to the Abbasid usurpation of Umayyad authority. This report offers Muhammad's response to a query about how to respond to an unjust ruler. The Prophet tells his followers not to rise up against a ruler whom they find loathesome as long as he allows Muslim prayers to continue. This is a common *hadith*, conveyed by a wide variety of transmitters. It has been interpreted in myriad ways by both medieval and modern scholars, even to provide justification for living under non-Muslim rule as long as prayer is allowed. In al-Awza'i's time, *hadith* reports such as this forbade revolts under virtually any circumstances and provided justification for autocratic rule, even by immoral, hated leaders. As long as a ruler did not banish Muslim prayer, God and his Prophet demanded loyalty to him. For al-Awza'i, this *hadith* is especially important for three reasons. First, it justifies, even commands, loyalty to al-Walid b. Yazid despite his spectacular moral failings. For all of his lewdness and cruelty, he did not prevent normal Muslim prayer and worship. His rule was destined by God and he at least maintained the bare minimum requirements for his legitimacy.

Second, the *hadith* justifies the condemnation of the Qadarite rebels who, for all of their purported piety, acted in defiance of the Prophet's command that they accept any ruler who did not infringe upon Muslim prayer. Finally, the *hadith* justifies al-Awza'i's own passive response to the Abbasids. They may have been usurpers, inspired by heretics, and they may have been genealogically deficient. Despite this, they did allow the proper practice of the religion to continue. Consequently, one could grouse about them and avoid serving them, but one could not rebel against them.

The reports discussed here are but a tiny portion of the corpus of *hadith* and other material transmitted by al-Awza'i. Most of his corpus addresses more mundane concerns and practical legal matters, such as prayer rituals, warfare and the division of spoils, commerce and rent, and inheritance. It is important to remember that material with direct political significance makes up a small portion of al-Awza'i's transmissions. However, the reports discussed here underscore his attitude toward important political matters, especially the relationship between ruler and ruled. These reports justify Umayyad autocracy, emphasize predestinarian dogma, and implicitly condemn al-Awza'i's Qadarite foes. At the same time, they emphasize the preordained role of the Arab elite and command loyalty to al-Awza'i's Umayyad patrons, including even the proudly immoral al-Walid. Combined, these reports also explain how al-Awza'i concluded that the murder of al-Walid was such a turning point for Islamic history, the end of the good old days of autocratic rule by pure Arabs predestined by God. Finally, it is important to note that these reports and the doctrinal positions they illustrate were entirely compatible with al-Awza'i's legal opinions, which gave great deference to those in positions of authority.

SURVIVING THE FALL OF THE UMAYYADS AND THE ABBASID REVOLUTION

Given his status as one of Hisham's confidants, it is remarkable that al-Awza'i somehow avoided becoming entangled in the political conflicts surrounding Hisham's succession. Before Hisham acceded to the caliphate, he had taken an oath to his brother and predecessor Yazid b. 'Abd al-Malik (r. 101/720–105/724), naming Yazid's son al-Walid as his own successor. This succession arrangement marked an important transition for the Umayyad dynasty, because it would mark the end of a long period of rule by sons of 'Abd al-Malik. Al-Walid was one of many members of the next generation who had caliphal aspirations. Yazid's maneuvering ensured that his son, rather than one of his many cousins, would be the first caliph of the new generation. During Hisham's lengthy reign, doubts surfaced about al-Walid's suitability to be the next caliph. Other Umayyad family members, perhaps out of jealousy and ambition as much as pious concern, objected to al-Walid's penchant for cruelty and his contempt toward them. Religious scholars were alarmed by al-Walid's shockingly public immoral behavior. While other Umayyad elites certainly engaged in their share of hedonistic distractions, they at least did so discreetly. Some scholars found the possibility of a caliph who flaunted his debauchery distressing for both the empire and the faith. Finally, Hisham himself wished that he could turn the empire over to his own son Maslama (hardly a pious exemplar himself), instead of al-Walid.

Some of Hisham's advisers urged him to repudiate al-Walid and declare Maslama or some other candidate to be his successor instead. Al-Walid's shortcomings were numerous and obvious, and his antipathy toward Hisham was a threat to those in his inner circle. It was not difficult to portray the possible succession of al-Walid as a calamity for the empire and for the religious authority of the caliphal office. However, Hisham's oath to his brother, some twenty years earlier, presented a formidable obstacle to any change of succession. The oath was unconditional and legally valid by all accounts. A sacred oath could not be broken lightly, especially by the caliph himself. Given that he was seen as a religious exemplar, his disregard for an oath could be used to degrade the force of oaths in general. Some scholars, including most notably al-Zuhri, argued that al-Walid's conduct was so egregious that it justified, even necessitated, that the oath be set aside for the good of the community. Others rejected this view and insisted that the oath remained binding regardless of al-Walid's faults. Those supporting the oath ultimately prevailed and those who had opposed al-Walid suffered his enmity after his accession.

It is curious that discussions of this explosive conflict include no mention of al-Awza'i or of his position on the matter. He surely took part in these debates, given his status as a prominent legal scholar and caliphal adviser. It seems most likely that he was one of those who advocated against breaking the oath to empower al-Walid. After al-Walid became caliph, he sought revenge against those who had tried to undermine his accession, even imprisoning some of his Umayyad kinsmen. He purportedly lamented that al-Zuhri had died before he came to power, denying him the opportunity to punish the famous scholar for his opposition. Al-Awza'i attracted no such condemnation from al-Walid, suggesting that he was not among those trying to deny al-Walid the caliphate. It is more plausible that al-Awza'i was instead one of the scholars who convinced Hisham to abide by his oath. Despite his bad behavior, of which al-Awza'i was surely aware, al-Walid remained the properly appointed successor to Hisham. His acceptance of al-Walid is consistent with al-Awza'i's views as described in other contexts. Al-Walid, like al-Awza'i, held staunchly predestinarian views. He had a noble Arab pedigree. The end of his brief reign marked the end of the living tradition.

Despite his recognition of al-Walid's legitimacy, al-Awza'i apparently ended his association with the caliphal court after Hisham's death. The exact date and circumstances of his retirement to Beirut are not described in his biographies. There is no indication that al-Walid dismissed him, but he was also apparently not asked to remain. This is not surprising, given that al-Walid immediately purged most of Hisham's retinue of officials and advisers. It is notable, however, that there is no suggestion of a rupture between al-Walid and al-Awza'i. Instead, al-Awza'i quietly withdrew to his ancestral homeland. Whether or not his retreat from political service was a subtle rebuke of al-Walid's behavior or policies is impossible to determine. His retirement was a peculiar choice, however. He was not yet forty years old and the recent death of his older colleague al-Zuhri would have cemented indisputably his status as the most prominent scholar in Damascus.

While there is no convincing indication that al-Awza'i ever returned to government service, there is an isolated but often repeated report that Yazid b. al-Walid attempted to appoint him as a *qadi*. In all likelihood, this report is a later fabrication. It is possible that Yazid reached out to al-Awza'i in an attempt to mend fences with Syrian elites whom his revolt had alienated. However, given al-Awza'i's hostility toward Yazid's Qadarite religious views and his insults to his Persian ancestry, such an effort would have been futile. More likely, the report is part of later hagiography about al-Awza'i, creating an opportunity for him to refuse government service and the office of *qadi* specifically. Later expectations that scholars avoid such entanglements made job offers and their rejection a common trope in biographies of great scholars. Assuming that the story is fictional, it is interesting and significant that its fabricator chose to describe al-Awza'i rebuffing the Qadarite Yazid rather than the libertine al-Walid. Regardless of the circumstances of his departure from Damascus, al-Awza'i clearly retained his prestige as a scholar and, as discussed below, spent much of his "retirement" offering legal advice and counsel to a wide array of clients.

AL-AWZA'I AND THE ABBASIDS

Al-Awza'i's relationship with the Abbasids is far better documented than are his Umayyad years. Biographical sources typically emphasize his post-revolutionary life, downplaying his links to the Umayyad regime earlier in life. Additionally, as will be seen below, many of the stories of his interactions with the Abbasids include themes of resistance to government service. Images of pious scholars standing up to worldly rulers became especially popular in biographies of scholars. It is possible that stories of al-Awza'i's interactions with the Abbasids are legendary to some degree. Such stories could have served to enhance al-Awza'i's reputation while distracting from his Umayyad connections and simultaneously explaining how he survived the revolution and retained his influence. Most of the reports appear as stories al-Awza'i shared with his followers and are not actually eyewitness accounts. Consequently, it is important to recognize that they could include a bit of boasting and dramatization for the sake of impressing his audience. At the same time, though, such self-promotion is incongruous with the typical image of al-Awza'i as a quiet, humble scholar.

There is no indication that al-Awza'i took part in either the revolution or in the messy Umayyad civil war that preceded it. He does not appear to have left Beirut, which was peripheral to both of these conflicts, until after the revolution. While Beirut was not an active theater in the intra-Muslim disputes of the 130s/740s, it was still considered a frontier zone. Beirut served as a staging area for raids against the Byzantines, by both land and sea. Al-Awza'i offered legal advice regarding such raids, but not about fighting between Muslims. He somehow avoided being drawn into the fray in any capacity.

There is also no indication that he served or advised the last Umayyad caliphs in any way. His antipathy toward Yazid and his brother and successor, Ibrahim, made it unlikely that he would assist them, even if they had requested it. The last Umayyad ruler, Marwan b. Muhammad, was a different matter, however. Like al-Awza'i, he was strictly predestinarian and sought to restore the rightful order by avenging al-Walid and placing his sons and chosen heirs in power. In many ways, he and al-Awza'i seem like natural allies, despite Marwan's non-Arab mother. However, there is no indication that Marwan sought al-Awza'i's advice or assistance, or that al-Awza'i offered any aid. This may have been a product of circumstances rather than a deliberate choice. Marwan spent his entire reign dealing with the military catastrophe of Yazid's civil war, trying to suppress an evolving array of factions within the Umayyad family and challengers from without, even before the Abbasids struck. Legal and theological issues would not have been his focus and al-Awza'i could offer little aid with military strategy. Deliberately or otherwise, al-Awza'i stayed on the sidelines during the years of turmoil and bloodshed following Hisham's death.

After the revolution, the newly ensconced Abbasids were suspicious of al-Awza'i despite his abstention from the struggle. His previous ties to the Umayyads made him a subject of Abbasid scrutiny. Fortunately for al-Awza'i, he was far enough removed from the Umayyad inner circle to avoid an invitation to the infamous post-revolutionary banquet at Nahr Abi Futrus, where some eighty prominent Umayyads were slaughtered. Instead, he was subjected to questioning by Abbasid officials testing his loyalty to, or at least acceptance of, the new regime. There are two clusters of stories about his encounters with early Abbasid officials. One set of reports involves an interrogation by 'Abdallah b. 'Ali (d. 147/764), the first Abbasid governor of Syria. The second cluster describes a later audience with the caliph al-Mansur. The accounts are dramatic, infused with hagiographic embellishments that glorify al-Awza'i. As mentioned above, they are also told from al-Awza'i's perspective, raising some doubts about their accuracy. Despite this, these stories offer useful insights into al-Awza'i's relationship with the Abbasids and his justification for his choices during and after the revolution. Their religious content is also consistent with other descriptions of al-Awza'i's views.

Al-Awza'i's interrogation by 'Abdallah b. 'Ali, reported most completely by Ibn 'Asakir, took place shortly after the revolution, likely in the Syrian city of Hama, where 'Abdallah held court. Some reports suggest that the meeting took place in the immediate aftermath of the massacre at Nahr Abi Futrus, describing the governor still holding the bloody club with which he had bludgeoned Umayyad leaders to death. Some sources specifically called the encounter a *mihna*, or inquisition, a term that evokes images of later Abbasid persecutions of scholars whose views they deemed aberrant. 'Abdallah summoned al-Awza'i to Hama and he complied, despite knowing the peril he faced.

The questions al-Awza'i faced in this encounter focus on three topics of religious and legal significance. 'Abdallah asks if it was legal to kill the Umayyads, if the Abbasids could take control of their property, and if the Prophet Muhammad had appointed his cousin 'Ali b. Abi Talib as his successor. Each of these topics was potentially explosive, particularly in the immediate aftermath of the revolution and 'Abdallah's slaughter of the Umayyads. In response, al-Awza'i is both defiant and elusive. Regarding the slaughter of the Umayyads, he declined to answer directly. Instead, he recited the three circumstances in which a Muslim's blood can legally be shed: as punishment for murder, apostasy, and in certain instances of adultery. He conveniently did not mention whether or not the Umayyads fit into any of these categories. There are several incompatible versions of al-Awza'i's judgment regarding Umayyad property. One response makes property legally owned by the Umayyads licit for the Abbasids to take. Others say that only property illegally held by the Umayyads could be taken. Still others indicate that illegally held Umayyad property would remain illegal for the Abbasids to claim. These confusing, apparently contradictory answers have a variety of implications regarding both property rights and Abbasid legitimacy, none of which is ideal from 'Abdallah's perspective. Each response, however, deflects the argument to focus on whether or not the Umayyads held their property legally. Either answer would have created difficulties for Abbasid claims either to property or to the legitimacy of their cause.

The question concerning Muhammad's designation of 'Ali is especially interesting. It is one of the few instances in which any reference to 'Ali or to 'Alids more generally appears in reports about al-Awza'i. While 'Alids were certainly part of the sectarian landscape during his time, al-Awza'i remained largely silent about them. The question is also important because during and immediately after the revolution, the Abbasids themselves claimed to be the beneficiaries of 'Ali's designation. Denying the designation would mean denying the principal foundation for Abbasid legitimacy. Al-Awza'i's response is both cleverly evasive and consistent with his own views. He simply tells 'Abdallah that none could have stopped 'Ali if he had been God's chosen leader. His answer is firmly predestinarian, denies 'Alid claims, and implies that later leaders, including the Umayyads, were assigned by God. Conveniently, al-Awza'i leaves open the possibility that the eventual rise of the Abbasids might also have been foreordained.

Al-Awza'i does not answer the questions put to him directly, but in the process he sets traps for 'Abdallah, forcing him to make difficult choices if he were to continue his interrogation. Were the Umayyads apostates? Did they legally own their property? Why did 'Ali lose if he was appointed by God? Answering any of these questions might restrict Abbasid options while allowing al-Awza'i to lure his opponent into contradictions. The techniques al-Awza'i uses here are similar to those he used against Ghaylan when his role was prosecutor rather than prosecuted. His answers are also consistent with his own doctrinal views. 'Abdallah apparently recognized the consequences of continuing the debate and demurred from doing so, implying that he too was familiar with al-Awza'i's argumentation techniques and could foresee how the chess game would play out. Rather than admitting defeat, 'Abdallah simply released al-Awza'i, apparently either satisfied that he was not a threat or convinced that further debate would produce a different, potentially greater threat. There are contradictory reports about whether or not 'Abdallah offered al-Awza'i a hefty stipend and whether or not he accepted.

The encounter with al-Mansur has a different tone and al-Awza'i uses slightly different techniques in this episode. It is not clear if stories involving al-Mansur are an alternative to those in which 'Abdallah appears, or if they represent a second direct encounter between al-Awza'i and the Abbasid authorities. Any meeting between al-Awza'i and al-Mansur would have taken place after the initial chaos of the revolution had passed. The encounter likely occurred either in 136/754 or 140/757, the only times when al-Mansur passed through Syria. Some reports begin with al-Awza'i congratulating al-Mansur on his accession to the caliphate, suggesting the 136/754 date and also implying that al-Awza'i accepted his legitimacy.

The content of the encounter is also different. Rather than an interrogation about Abbasid legitimacy, the dialogue consists largely of al-Awza'i admonishing the caliph and warning about the consequences of tyranny and greed. Al-Awza'i's comments are upsetting enough that one of al-Mansur's aides reaches for his sword at one point, only to be deterred by the caliph. Al-Awza'i uses three different techniques to insulate himself from retribution for his criticism. Unlike his exchange with 'Abdallah, this performance is infused with citations from *hadith* and Qur'an. Al-Mansur cannot object to such citations, particularly since they do not explicitly apply to him or his regime. Al-Awza'i chooses his examples carefully, focusing on earlier holy figures who were subject to criticism. He reminds al-Mansur that King David was chastised and that even the Prophet Muhammad himself received a scolding from the angel Gabriel when he behaved badly. If the most esteemed religious leaders of the past, recognized as God's prophets, were imperfect and subject to censure, a lesser figure like al-Mansur could not be immune to criticism. Al-Awza'i's final technique is especially clever.

He repeatedly cites exegetical reports from 'Abdallah b. al-'Abbas (d. 67/687), the esteemed companion of the Prophet, who also happened to be al-Mansur's great-grandfather. Al-Awza'i emphasizes this lineage, beginning his citations with "your grandfather said ..." By relying heavily on *hadith* and Qur'an, along with the authority of the Abbasids' fore-father, and by reminding al-Mansur that every leader and prophet is sub-ject to scrutiny and criticism, al-Awza'i makes it difficult for al-Mansur to object to his admonitions. Following the example of 'Abdallah b. 'Ali in the previous interrogation, al-Mansur opts not to respond, offering al-Awza'i a stipend and sending him on his way.

While these stories of al-Awza'i's interactions with Abbasid author-ities likely contain legendary elements that burnish al-Awza'i's repu-tation, they still offer important insights into both his beliefs and his political status. It is important to note that stories of these encounters do not deny or obscure al-Awza'i's connections to the defeated Umayyad regime. Indeed, his interrogation by 'Abdallah b. 'Ali occurred because of his ties to the Umayyads. Other religious scholars who were less closely associated with the Umayyads were spared such traumatic inqui-sitions. These stories serve an important purpose in al-Awza'i's biogra-phies by explaining his survival after the revolution, despite his close ties to the Umayyad regime. Al-Awza'i neither denies his connections to the Umayyads nor condemns his previous patrons. He only begrudgingly accepts the Abbasids, yet he gains their respect as well. These stories also become the foundation for the standard narrative of scholarly resis-tance to political authority. Like other scholars, al-Awza'i is later por-trayed as opposed to or at least indifferent to political authorities. Here, the pious scholar stands before the ruler, threatened with death, and holds his ground. The Abbasid authorities' decision not to engage in fur-ther arguments or punish al-Awza'i, an implicit admission of defeat, also helps to explain why al-Awza'i retained his influence despite his past.

AL-AWZA'I'S POST-REVOLUTIONARY LIFE

After leaving government service behind and extracting himself from potential Abbasid retaliation, al-Awza'i spent his remaining days in

Beirut. He was still relatively young when he retreated to Beirut, and his residence there lasted for some thirty years. It is not clear whether or not he left the city for any purpose after his arrival. He may have ventured to the Byzantine frontier on occasion, but the sources are not explicit about this. There is also no indication of how he funded his retirement in Beirut. Some reports suggest that he received stipends from the Abbasids, while others portray him refusing their money. He had been entered into the *diwan* as a result of his service as a young man, but it is not clear whether or not the Abbasids continued to pay pensions granted by the Umayyads. He had no family wealth to fall back on, so he must have had some other source of income in Beirut. It is possible that he accepted payment for legal advice, although the sources do not mention such arrangements.

It is perhaps a misnomer to call his Beirut years a retirement. He continued to engage in legal discourse on a variety of matters during this period. As mentioned above, Beirut was a frontier zone from which raids on the Byzantines were launched. Al-Awza'i's expertise in military law would have been in demand in such a setting. Some of his responses to legal queries allude to specific campaigns on the frontier during this period, confirming that he continued to offer his advice after he left Damascus. It is unclear whether or not he was compensated for his efforts. It is also likely that al-Awza'i composed his lost legal and theological works during his time in Beirut. In addition to his legal works, he also purportedly wrote a refutation of the Qadarite Thawr b. Yazid (d. *c.* 150/767) with whom he had sparred after the revolution. Some sources also mention exchanges of letters and books with Sufyan al-Thawri and others, though they do not preserve any of the actual letters or even offer clear descriptions of their content.

The most significant surviving product of al-Awza'i's Beirut years is a series of letters he wrote to Abbasid officials. Ibn Abi Hatim (d. 327/938) reproduced ten of these letters and a smattering are repeated in other sources as well. There are reports of additional letters, though the letters themselves are not extant. This collection of correspondence is an unusual trove of information about life on the frontier and about al-Awza'i and his continuing influence. Letters are common in historical sources and chronicles, though their authenticity is almost always debated and they are often seen as literary devices used to drive the historical narrative or to elucidate relationships between historical actors. Such epistolary accretions are not unique to the Arabic sources, but are a common feature of medieval and ancient historical writing.

Al-Awzaʻi's letters are atypical. Most letters in historical sources are either meant for public proclamations of official policy, or are correspondence between officials, adding detail to the narrative and sometimes explaining peculiar twists. Some letters in Arabic sources, such as those ascribed to al-Walid b. Yazid, are actually elaborate treatises presented in epistolary form. Al-Awzaʻi's letters do not fit any of these categories. Instead, they are intercessions on behalf of local, often unidentified people mostly dwelling on the frontier. They are addressed to officials at different levels of the Abbasid hierarchy and focus on local events and communities, some of which were not momentous enough to merit mention in the chronicles at all. They offer glimpses into the realities of frontier life, evidence of the peculiarities of the administrative power structure, and underscore al-Awzaʻi's continuing reputation and influence. Because of their unusual features, most scholars accept their authenticity, despite their general skepticism about letters in historical sources.

The letters address a variety of subjects, which include pleas for increased stipends for those stationed on the frontier, requests for prisoners to be released, objections to improper distributions of spoils, and admonishments for harsh treatment of local Christian populations. Three of the most interesting letters are entreaties on behalf of the people of Qaliqala. This was a small border outpost in Armenia near modern Erzurum. The fortress had fallen to the Byzantines sometime between 133/751 and 137/755 and many Muslim soldiers and civilians remained captives there. Stories of abuse, forced conversion, and the enslavement and defilement of Muslim women spread as far as Beirut, but Abbasid leaders had made little effort either to retake the stronghold or to ransom the captives to save them from further harm. Their plight obviously moved al-Awzaʻi, who wrote three intensive pleas for Qaliqala's relief. He sent one letter to the caliph himself, another to ʻIsa b. ʻAli, the caliph's uncle and adviser, and a third to

Sulayman b. al-Mujalid, who was al-Mansur's constant companion. He informs the latter two that he has written to the caliph and urges their intercession on the prisoners' behalf. One of the letters also alludes to previous correspondence about this issue. Unfortunately, there is no indication of whether or not al-Awza'i's entreaties were successful.

These and the other letters demonstrate that al-Awza'i remained an effective advocate whose support both his neighbors and people farther afield sought out. He was someone who could influence local officials, regional governors, and even the caliph himself. Despite his physical distance from Baghdad, he knew whom to approach when the caliph needed extra prodding to respond to al-Awza'i's concerns. The letters also underscore al-Awza'i's understanding of social hierarchies. His letters to the caliph are filled with deference and praise, while those to local officials are less diplomatic, and even harsh in tone. His letters to al-Mahdi are especially interesting. Al-Awza'i wrote to al-Mahdi on at least two occasions, once asking for mercy for an unnamed group of prisoners, and a second time seeking increased stipends for the people of Mecca, who were suffering from shortages and high prices. Two things stand out about these letters. First, they were written to al-Mahdi while he was heir apparent, seeking his intervention with the caliph. This suggests that the caliph's son had a degree of influence over his father and that the heir apparent himself was a center of power in Baghdad. Second, the tone of these letters remains deferential, but is also less formal than that in the letters to the caliph. There are subtle hints that al-Awza'i's relationship with al-Mahdi was friendlier than with other Abbasid leaders. An isolated report in Ibn 'Asakir describes another interaction between al-Awza'i and al-Mahdi that also suggests that their relationship was more cordial. In this account, al-Mahdi inquires about al-Awza'i's refusal to wear black, the color representing the Abbasids. The gist of al-Awza'i's lengthy, almost ill-tempered reply was that he simply did not like black. His response inspired laughter rather than anger from al-Mahdi. Al-Awza'i's response may have been entirely disingenuous, since there are other reports that he donned black during the reign of Yazid b. al-Walid, perhaps in protest against his governor Ibn Suraqa. Apparently, al-Mahdi was unaware of this or sufficiently enamored with al-Awza'i that he overlooked his past wardrobe choices.

Had al-Awza'i survived to see al-Mahdi accede to the caliphate, one wonders if he might have returned to the caliph's inner circle. It is also interesting to note that al-Mahdi differed in one significant way from the other caliphs who ruled after al-Awza'i's retirement. His mother was a free Arab of noble lineage. If al-Awza'i really was guided by the *hadith* lamenting the rise of sons of foreign slaves, al-Mahdi may have represented a restoration of the proper order in his mind.

CONCLUSION: EVALUATING AL-AWZA'I AS A POLITICAL FIGURE

Despite efforts in later sources to obscure al-Awza'i's political involvement, it is clear that he was not averse to entanglements with government officials. While ill-defined, his role under the Umayyads was one of intimate engagement with the ruling elite. He advised the caliph Hisham and assisted him in important, even public ways, as evidenced by his prosecution of Ghaylan al-Dimashqi, the most prominent heretic of his time. He did not have a specific title, and does not appear to have sought one, but he served the regime openly and without reservation. His role under the Abbasids was less direct but still important. From Beirut, he served as an advocate for those seeking redress from the government. He did not work for the Abbasids, but rather worked to persuade them to act appropriately. Whether or not those for whom he advocated were paying clients is unclear. The fact that they engaged al-Awza'i to argue on their behalf demonstrates that he was still seen to have significant influence.

Al-Awza'i's attitude toward government service generally and individual leaders specifically was complex, but ultimately consistent. He did not object to scholarly service to government per se. He was simply selective about whom to serve and how to do so. Service to the Umayyads, whom he saw as legitimate caliphs, at least until the murder of al-Walid, was perfectly acceptable. Service to usurping Qadarites of dubious lineage was not. As for the Abbasids, al-Awza'i refused to serve them directly, but avoided alienating them entirely. Consequently, he could continue to appeal to them on behalf of others.

In his interactions with ruling elites, al-Awza'i displayed pragmatic political savvy. At times he was deferential, while at other times he was confrontational. He clearly understood the subtleties required to navigate the social and political hierarchies of the two caliphates and knew how to placate the egos of those whose assistance he needed without himself becoming a sycophant. Despite his reputation as a pious, detached scholar, al-Awza'i knew how to play political games and did so deftly.

One noteworthy aspect of his political involvement is the diversity of those who sought his aid after his retreat to Beirut. Both Christians and Muslims from the Beirut area appealed to al-Awza'i for help in dealing with Abbasid mistreatment. He wrote on behalf of people as far away as Mecca seeking relief from their suffering, and devoted extraordinary effort to advocate for the victims at Qaliqala, who were on a distant frontier and had no obvious connection to al-Awza'i or to his Beirut environs. It is remarkable that prisoners in Armenia, Muslim residents in Mecca, and local Christians all relied upon a retired Umayyad legal scholar in Beirut as their advocate. Respect for al-Awza'i clearly extended far beyond greater Syria, and his reputation for successful advocacy must have exceeded that of more local scholars whom those in need could have more easily engaged.

Historians, both medieval and modern, have generally overlooked the extent of al-Awza'i's political involvement and influence. The standard image of the pious early Muslim scholar was one of political detachment and disdain for the trappings of power and wealth. Stories of al-Awza'i's initial confrontations with the Abbasids provide ample evidence around which scholars could build a narrative of political resistance. However, a closer look at the material demands a more nuanced understanding of al-Awza'i's attitude toward and experience with politics. While he objected to the Abbasid revolution, he had willingly served certain Umayyads and eventually came to a modus vivendi with the new regime that allowed him to advocate on behalf of those who needed him. His survival of the revolution and his continuing influence are extraordinary and indicate that al-Awza'i was more politically astute and pragmatic than previous portrayals suggest.

6

AL-AWZA'I'S LEGACY

Evaluating the enduring impact of a "failed" *madhhab* and its eponym is a difficult task. While al-Awza'i's students appreciated his teachings and applied his methods, they did not form a cohesive school that could endure for more than a few decades. Consequently, as the previous chapters have noted, al-Awza'i's views are less well preserved than those of some of his contemporaries. Nor did any of his students appear to produce extensive explications of his methods, a crucial element for the survival of a legal *madhhab*. As a result, al-Awza'i's legal approach and theological views could easily be appropriated by others, or in some cases simply forgotten. Conversely, the failure of his followers to continue his tradition also meant that the elements of his views that have been preserved are likely free of later accretions and may represent the legal and theological landscape of his time more accurately than the more embellished textual records of his contemporaries.

Despite the fact that his legal *madhhab* was short-lived, al-Awza'i remains an important figure in early Islamic thought. As a scholar who apparently wrote very little, who was associated with a collapsed political dynasty, and who did not attract an enduring cadre of students, al-Awza'i could easily have faded into obscurity. The fact that his influence and memory endure underscores his significance. His legacy persisted through several important students, the persistence of his influence in certain key regions, and in works on legal matters. In addition, there has been a resurgence in interest in al-Awza'i's views in modern times.

AL-AWZA'I'S STUDENTS

Biographical sources typically include long lists of students who purportedly studied under al-Awza'i's direction. Each of these lists includes dozens of names, with the total number of students attributed to al-Awza'i easily exceeding one hundred. There is nothing unusual about either the lists or their lengths. The *muhaddiths* and critics who produced the biographical sources needed to account for who studied with whom in order to evaluate *isnads* in *hadith* transmissions. While the lists include an impressive array of scholars, some of whom became far more famous than al-Awza'i, not all of these were his disciples. Many were more interested in *hadith* than in legal methods or theology. Repeating these lists and commenting on those who appear therein will not offer much insight into al-Awza'i's legacy. Instead, it is more productive to focus on a few students who were more closely associated with al-Awza'i and his views, who also transmitted significant quantities of material from al-Awza'i, and whose focus was not entirely on *hadith*.

Arguably, the most famous and important of al-Awza'i's students was 'Abd al-Razzaq al-San'ani (d. 211/826). 'Abd al-Razzaq was a noted Yemeni scholar who traveled to Beirut specifically to study with al-Awza'i. It is important to note that 'Abd al-Razzaq was born in or around 126/744, after al-Awza'i had retreated to Beirut. He likely went there to study with al-Awza'i at least twenty years after al-Awza'i's withdrawal from political life. The fact that a promising young scholar would undertake such a journey to learn from al-Awza'i underscores his continuing prestige as an authority. It also illustrates that his past association with the Umayyad regime had not tainted his reputation. 'Abd al-Razzaq went on to produce the *Musannaf*, one of the earliest collections of *hadith* material. In this groundbreaking work he included significant material from al-Awza'i, and even more from al-Awza'i's comrade Sufyan al-Thawri, who had traveled to Yemen after the Abbasid revolution. 'Abd al-Razzaq's collection marked the pinnacle of Yemeni *hadith* scholarship. After its circulation widened, scholars no longer bothered to travel to Yemen to study. 'Abd al-Razzaq's collection and evaluation of Yemeni scholarship was considered to be so thorough that nothing more could be learned in his homeland. His book was an acceptable substitute for travel. In addition to his impact on *hadith* scholarship, 'Abd al-Razzaq also greatly influenced Ibn Hanbal (d. 241/855), the eponymous founder of the Hanbali *madhhab*, and his followers. 'Abd al-Razzaq's determination to seek out and include material from al-Awza'i in his work may have contributed to the respect the Hanbalis exhibited toward al-Awza'i as well.

Muhammad b. Yusuf al-Firyabi (d. 212/827), another noted *muhaddith*, also traveled to Beirut specifically to study with al-Awza'i. Like 'Abd al-Razzaq, he was a widely traveled *hadith* scholar and critic who sought al-Awza'i's expertise after the Abbasid revolution. He too was a teacher of Ibn Hanbal and a student of al-Awza'i's colleague Sufyan al-Thawri. He appears frequently as a transmitter in the major *hadith* collections. While he does not appear to have been a native Syrian, al-Firyabi ultimately settled in Qaysariya where he continued to teach. His son was also an important scholar who wrote a well-known work praising the merits of Jerusalem. Al-Firyabi's decision to seek out al-Awza'i as a teacher and to remain in Syria illustrates both al-Awza'i's continued prominence and the enduring importance of Syria as a scholarly center.

Abu Ishaq al-Fazari (d. ca. 185/802) was the student most closely associated with al-Awza'i. He was also the most important of his generation of "frontier scholars" who provided legal advice to those defending the borderlands against Byzantine incursions. A native of Kufa, al-Fazari spent most of his life on the frontier, based in the much-contested city of Massisa. He was a student of al-Awza'i and Sufyan al-Thawri and recorded their opinions on a wide variety of warfare-related topics in his *Kitab al-siyar*. He also followed his mentor in his antipathy toward the Qadarites, whom he argued should be barred from the frontier. Al-Fazari's *Kitab al-siyar* was one of the earliest and most important works on the laws of war and it greatly influenced later works in the genre. Given the extent to which he relied on al-Awza'i, whom he cited constantly, it is possible that al-Fazari's work largely mirrors his mentor's lost work on the same subject. Al-Fazari's work was widely read and remains the most important repository of al-Awza'i's opinions on warfare, for which he is best remembered.

Al-Awza'i had many other famous and influential students. As a group, they had wide geographical origins. Most appear to have been primarily *hadith* scholars, though the tendency of later sources to reimagine early Islamic legal scholars as *muhaddiths* may overemphasize this aspect of al-Awza'i's legacy. As the legal landscape changed during the century following al-Awza'i's death, many of those who had an affinity for al-Awza'i either joined other *madhhabs* or later had their memories appropriated by other *madhhabs*. This process appears to have varied by region, to some extent.

AL-AWZA'I'S REGIONAL PERSISTENCE

Al-Awza'i's students hailed from all regions of the Muslim world. Many were from his native Syria or remained there after journeying there to study, to spend time on the Byzantine frontier, or both. Others, such as 'Abd al-Razzaq al-San'ani, traveled to Syria to study and then returned to their homelands, or continued their quests for knowledge in other scholarly centers.

It is not surprising that al-Awza'i's influence persisted longest in his native Syria. After all, Syria was his homeland, and those who wished to study under his guidance had to seek him there. Syria was also the core of Umayyad territory and Damascus had a long scholarly tradition that predated Islam. Some of al-Awza'i's students continued to serve the Abbasids in various capacities, despite al-Awza'i's association with the Umayyads and his own reticence about serving the new regime. However, within a generation or so, they were slowly supplanted by scholars associated with more vibrant *madhhabs*. This was not the end of al-Awza'i's legacy in Syria, though. A century after his death, interest in his life and thought experienced a resurgence of sorts. A growing emphasis on historical writing combined with parochial Syrian pride made al-Awza'i an attractive subject for scholars seeking to reclaim and remember the glorious past of Damascus and Syria generally. This trend began with the works of the Syrian historian Abu Zur'a (d. 281/894) and continued somewhat unevenly for several centuries, culminating with the monumental city history of

Ibn 'Asakir (d. 571/1176). While these works may include hagiographic embellishments, the meticulous fidelity their authors showed toward earlier sources has been demonstrated by modern studies. The mere fact that al-Awza'i, rather than other Syrian scholars of his era, features prominently in such works underscores his importance and suggests that he had not faded into obscurity before being rediscovered by the likes of Ibn 'Asakir. It is also not surprising that interest in al-Awza'i and his legal thought experienced a resurgence during the era of the Crusades. For the first time in centuries, the whole of Syria found itself on the frontier between Muslim and Christian forces. The complex, tedious details of military law that were al-Awza'i's expertise were especially relevant again. Despite his continuing importance in Syria, there are no indications that al-Awza'i's *madhhab* experienced a revival. He remained a trusted authority on particular topics, but was not seen as the architect of an overarching set of legal theories. Other *madhhabs*, especially the Shafi'is, had become too entrenched for the reintroduction of an older school as a potential rival, even if the al-Awza'i school had survived long enough to articulate more comprehensive methods.

Al-Awza'i's influence also persisted for some time in al-Andalus. The Iberian Peninsula was beyond the reach of the Abbasid revolution and continued to be ruled by members of the Umayyad family, specifically descendants of Hisham b. 'Abd al-Malik whom al-Awza'i had served. In addition, Umayyad loyalists who refused to submit to Abbasid rule found refuge there after the revolution. It is not surprising that this constituency included some of al-Awza'i's students. His most prominent disciple in al-Andalus was Sa'sa'a b. Sallam al-Shami (d. 192/807), a Syrian scholar who resided in Cordoba and advised the Umayyad rulers there. Cordoba is also the site of al-Awza'i's most visible impact on Umayyad Spain. When plans were being made to expand the central mosque in Cordoba, Sa'sa'a famously consulted al-Awza'i regarding the proposal to plant fruit trees in the courtyard. Modern tourists can thank al-Awza'i for the shady respite the courtyard trees still provide on hot summer days. It is likely that the continued prominence of al-Awza'i in al-Andalus stemmed from more than mere Umayyad nostalgia or a yearning for shade. The complicated situation of the Iberian frontier was remarkably similar to that in Syria during al-Awza'i's time. Control of territory constantly changed, alliances shifted, property was taken and retaken, local populations and leaders converted to and from Islam (sometimes repeatedly), and diplomacy between Muslim and Christian potentates was essential. Al-Awza'i's expertise on the laws of war covered precisely these circumstances and had a practical, immediate applicability in al-Andalus. The fact that al-Awza'i 's followers, including Sa'sa'a and others, were able to consult directly with al-Awza'i suggests that a network of scholarly communication continued to function between Cordoba and Beirut despite the political turmoil in the territory between. The combina-tion of these factors explains why al-Awza'i and his work remained popular in Muslim Spain, despite the fact that he himself had never set foot there.

The decline of al-Awza'i's influence in al-Andalus is more difficult to interpret. In the late second/eighth to early third/ninth century, al-Awza'i's *madhhab* was rapidly eclipsed by the Malikis. The reasons for this transition are murky and explanations tend to be speculative and not especially satisfying. None of them involve legal matters directly. Some speculate that the Umayyad rulers in Cordoba chose to follow Maliki law to emphasize ties to Medina for propaganda purposes. Some point to the rising prominence of a cadre of Maliki merchants in the capital as the impetus for the shift. Others point to the personal preferences of Hisham b. 'Abd al-Rahman (r. 172/788–180/796). Despite the official embrace of the Malikis, al-Awza'i retained a fol-lowing and a degree of popularity. Nearly a century after al-Awza'i's death, and decades after the rise of Malikism in Umayyad Spain, the noted Andalusi scholar al-A'naqi (d. 262/876) penned a work on the merits of al-Awza'i (*Fada'il al-Awza'i*). The fact that there was interest in and apparently an audience for such a work suggests that al-Awza'i's influence lingered longer than the abbreviated accounts in the chron-icles suggest. It is also worth noting that the fruit trees in the mosque at Cordoba remained, despite Maliki objections to such ornaments.

There is less evidence for al-Awza'i's legacy in the eastern Islamic lands. He does appear in legal and *hadith* texts compiled in the East, but does not appear to have had many followers there. This is not surprising, given the scholarly and political dynamics of the time. Khurasan and other eastern lands were the birthplace of the Abbasid movement and would have been less tolerant of Umayyad supporters, both before and after the revolution. Moreover, these territories were the intellectual stronghold of the Hanafis, al-Awza'i's fiercest rivals. Finally, al-Awza'i's colleague Sufyan al-Thawri had a stronger following in the East. Perhaps those who were amenable to al-Awza'i's ideas gravitated to Sufyan instead, given that he was less tainted by Umayyad association.

While al-Awza'i's continuing influence was geographically uneven, it remained significant, particularly in Syria and Iberia. The fact that he continued to attract followers and attention outside his Syrian homeland is especially important. This is an indication that he was not merely a regional authority, but instead had more universal appeal. This widespread appeal is also evident in his legal legacy, where he is not typically associated exclusively with Syria either.

AL-AWZA'I'S LEGAL LEGACY

Al-Awza'i is typically remembered as the leader of a failed *madhhab* that vanished shortly after his death and never achieved a significant following. To an extent, this description is accurate. However, it is also an oversimplified and anachronistic explanation. The main difficulty with this interpretation is that it presumes that the paradigm of eponymous *madhhab*s was in vogue earlier than the evidence suggests. It is difficult to evaluate the impact of a movement that failed, but even more so when it rose and fell during a time of epistemological fluidity.

Al-Awza'i was part of a larger, somewhat amorphous Umayyad legal tradition that was not necessarily attached to him by name. The practice of labeling legal traditions eponymously came somewhat later, at a time when al-Awza'i's followers were already dispersed, either as independent scholars who defied easy *madhhab* identification, or as adherents of the newly emerging eponymous groups. The dissolution of al-Awza'i's *madhhab*, such as it was, appears to have taken place over several generations. His immediate students were not identified with other *madhhab*s and were often only loosely connected to al-Awza'i in later sources. Scholars of the next generation, however, were more likely to be attached to other traditions. This suggests that whatever coherence al-Awza'i's followers felt waned after a few decades at most. It also reflects the growing importance of eponymous *madhhab* labels. Scholarly independence with vague connections to earlier figures like al-Awza'i was no longer common. Instead, affiliation to a recognized *madhhab* was the norm, and later generations of al-Awza'i's admirers conformed, rather than trying to sustain or revive their own al-Awza'i *madhhab*. This trajectory is consistent with prevalent understandings of the development of Islamic legal scholarship and networks. However, al-Awza'i and his students tend not to have been identified with regional traditions as some articulations of these developments would expect.

Later generations of al-Awza'i's followers tended to gravitate either to the Maliki or the Hanbali schools. The tendency to join the Malikis appears to be more prominent in al-Andalus and the West generally. Perhaps this reflects the popularity Malik enjoyed there, or perhaps it was simply a matter of political expediency. Others, particularly in Iraq, joined the emerging Hanbali school, possibly in solidarity with Ibn Hanbal's antipathy toward the Hanafis. Methodologically, either choice was defensible. Like al-Awza'i, Malik emphasized the normative force of community practice, though for Malik, the community to be emulated was more circumscribed, including only Medina and not the *umma* as a whole. For al-Awza'i's followers, this was not a great deviation from his method. Given that the longer, geographically broader living tradition al-Awza'i had accepted treated Umayyad leaders as exemplars, it would have been difficult for his followers not to restrict the scope of normative community practice after the Umayyads fell from grace. The Hanbali school was also a viable option for those who admired al-Awza'i. As discussed above, some of al-Awza'i's most prominent students excelled in *hadith* transmission and gained the respect of the nascent Hanbali movement. For those who remembered al-Awza'i as a *muhaddith*, the Hanbalis provided an agreeable home. For those followers of al-Awza'i who were more concerned with jurisprudence than with *hadith*, the contempt they and the Hanbalis shared for the Hanafis could serve as common ground, even though al-Awza'i was less emphatic in his rejection of personal opinion and analogy than Ibn Hanbal was. It goes without saying that few, if any of al-Awza'i's students or their successors joined the Hanafis. Surprisingly, connections between al-Awza'i's followers and the Shafi'i *madhhab* were quite rare, despite the eventual predominance of the Shafi'is in Syria. It is possible that al-Awza'i's followers had dispersed to other *madhhabs* before the Shafi'is gained influence in Damascus, or simply that they preferred the Malikis. This is a question that requires more investigation.

Given al-Awza'i's association with the Umayyads and his students' inability to create a cohesive, enduring tradition focused on his methods, it is not surprising that al-Awza'i's *madhhab* was short-lived. Changes in the political landscape and in conceptions of social organization among scholars precluded the creation of a sustained, institutionalized *madhhab*. However, al-Awza'i's students and their students remained important and influential. Some of his followers were absorbed by other *madhhabs*, but they continued to preserve and transmit his methods and specific legal solutions. This is evident in several discrete aspects of Islamic law where al-Awza'i continued to be treated as an authority and where his influence outweighed his following.

In particular, al-Awza'i continued to be cited as an authority on issues of warfare and related questions regarding taxation. These are topics to which al-Awza'i gave a great deal of attention during his days near the Byzantine frontier. They were also topics of great political importance. The division of spoils, land ownership, and taxation were of special interest to Abbasid leaders. It is worth noting that one of the topics about which al-Awza'i was interrogated in the aftermath of the revolution was the legality of Abbasid property seizures. During the Umayyad period he was arguably the most respected authority on such questions.

After the revolution, his views remained authoritative, but also irritating to the Abbasid caliphs. Shortly after the revolution, the Abbasids embraced rival Hanafi views on such issues, articulated primarily by Abu Hanifa's student Abu Yusuf. The contrast between their opinions on sometimes tedious, technical issues that still had fiscal implications for the Abbasids meant that al-Awza'i's opinions had to be engaged and rebutted to justify the Hanafi view. It is in this context that Abu Yusuf wrote his *Radd 'ala siyar al-Awza'i*, which meant to refute al-Awza'i's positions. Perhaps ironically, Abu Yusuf's work has actually become one of the principal repositories of al-Awza'i's opinions on warfare and taxation. Despite Hanafi efforts to dispose of al-Awza'i's views, they remained important, as evidenced by their extensive citation by al-Shafi'i (d. 205/820) in his *Kitab al-umm* and by al-Tabari in his *Ikhtilaf*. Later sources also continued to cite al-Awza'i regarding issues of warfare and taxation, illustrating the persistence of his influence on such topics.

As discussed earlier, al-Awza'i was also recognized as an important scholar of *hadith*. This is nothing extraordinary, as most reputable scholars of his era either trafficked in *hadith* or were transformed into *muhaddith*s by later biographical sources which tended to focus on *hadith* transmission as the principal mark of scholarly attainment. As a result of this tendency in the sources, al-Awza'i's interest and expertise in *hadith* may be overstated. He does, however, appear as a *hadith* transmitter in each of the canonical collections, though not as frequently as some of his colleagues such as Sufyan al-Thawri and al-Zuhri. In these compilations, he is universally treated as a respected source and the accuracy of his transmissions is not questioned. As mentioned above, he appears in collections compiled by scholars in the East as well as other regions, suggesting that his reputation as a *hadith* scholar was perhaps more widespread than his regard as a legal authority. More significantly, the *hadith* reports cover a broad array of topics, rather than just the military issues with which he is often associated. This illustrates that his interest was not confined to narrow topics related to the frontier, but that he instead pursued and transmitted knowledge on the full spectrum of legal and religious topics. Additionally, the fact that *hadith* reports transmitted on his authority continued to be cited over the centuries demonstrates that his reputation, at least as a *muhaddith*, did not diminish significantly over time.

Al-Awza'i also appears frequently in the voluminous works of comparative legal literature. This genre of works, known broadly as the *ikhtilaf al-fuqaha'*, or disagreements between scholars, catalogues legal opinions of important thinkers on important topics. The genre emerged fairly early, in the late second/eighth century, likely as handbooks to provide lists of acceptable answers to specific legal questions. They quickly grew to include more esoteric and hypothetical questions, as a means to showcase scholars' knowledge of legal minutiae. Some later works grew to dozens of volumes and likely were no longer useful as practical handbooks. Most were produced by scholars attached to specific legal schools who may have intended for them to emphasize their masters' superiority to rivals. However, these works seldom betray polemical agendas explicitly.

While none of these works was produced by al-Awza'i's students, he does appear in many of them, sometimes prominently. Here, as is the case with the *hadith* collections, al-Awza'i is cited on a wide array of topics. In fact, the majority of al-Awza'i citations in the *ikhtilaf* works focus on prayer and ritual rather than on the military topics for which he is more famous. Here again, his broad interests are represented. It is significant that, even in works written by followers of rival *madhhab*s, al-Awza'i is still cited. He does not appear either as a foil for refutation, or as a constant voice of affirmation for a particular scholar's views. Instead, he is treated as a respected, independent legal authority. This points to a continuing appreciation for his solutions to substantive legal questions, even centuries after the demise of his own *madhhab*.

Al-Awza'i's legal legacy remained despite the demise of his *madhhab* and the dispersal of his followers. He was still respected as a legal authority, even by scholars associated with other legal schools. While some of his views may have been appropriated by other *madhhab*s, and later generations of scholars associated with him joined the Malikis or Hanbalis, al-Awza'i retained his relevance as a legal authority on a broad array of topics.

AL-AWZA'I IN MODERN TIMES

In addition to his permanent place in the *hadith* collections and legal texts, al-Awza'i has been remembered and invoked in several new and interesting ways in modern times. Perhaps the most visible evidence of modern appreciation for al-Awza'i is his tomb on the outskirts of Beirut. The unassuming but well-maintained shrine attracts a modest but steady stream of visitors and pilgrims to this day. It is likely that al-Awza'i himself would not have approved of such veneration. Tomb visitation and prayers for saintly intercession carried the taint of idolatry for al-Awza'i and others of his era. Nonetheless, pilgrims still appear at his burial place for such purposes. His tomb and the activities surrounding it accentuate al-Awza'i's prominence in Beirut's historical memory.

Even centuries after his death, al-Awza'i is arguably the most important Muslim religious scholar associated with the city. While it is routine for a city to glorify famous people from its past out of civic pride and the desire to anchor the city's place in broader historical narratives, al-Awza'i is in many ways an appropriate figure for Beirut to emphasize in modern times. Elevating al-Awza'i serves to elevate Beirut's stature in the development of early Islam. The fact that al-Awza'i chose to abandon Damascus to return to his ancestral home may resonate with modern Lebanese national pride as well. In some ways, al-Awza'i is an idealistic Islamic symbol for Beirut. Reports of his legal work and stories of his advocacy for his neighbors portray a diverse environment in which Christians and Muslims mingled freely. Accounts of his funeral universally emphasize that large numbers of Christians, Jews, and Copts all joined al-Awza'i's fellow Muslims in the procession. Some even imply that non-Muslim prayers were said over him. The memory of the spectacle of an interfaith procession culminating with an ecumenical burial at al-Awza'i's tomb makes both the shrine and its occupant important symbols for a city that has vacillated between sectarian harmony and strife in modern times.

In addition to his parochial popularity in Beirut, al-Awza'i has also been deployed to represent broader agendas. Some modern scholars have focused on al-Awza'i's encounters with Abbasid authorities as examples of pious defiance in the face of tyrannical rulers. The persistence of secular, undemocratic, often despotic regimes in many Muslim countries has made exemplary tales of scholarly resistance a popular theme in both academic and popular works. Al-Awza'i's refusal to submit to ʿAbdallah b. ʿAli, Ibn Hanbal's defiance toward his Abbasid interlocutors, and other early Islamic examples provide models for contemporary dissidence. The contemporary use of such stories represents a curious intersection between modern political agendas and medieval hagiography.

Al-Awzaʿi also figures prominently in modern efforts to assert early Islamic origins for international law. In recent decades, the *siyar* literature has been read less as a catalogue of the laws of war and more as a set of rules governing the conduct of nations. The general argument is that modern international legal norms were actually derived from or at least foreshadowed in Islamic legal sources. There is material in the *siyar* literature that might be used to support such assertions. For instance, the *siyar* works describe in some detail the rules for military engagement and conduct. They describe who can initiate military operations and under what circumstances. They also place restrictions on conduct in combat, clarifying what constitutes an acceptable military target and addressing issues of collateral damage. For example, al-Awzaʿi and others emphasize that fruit orchards should be spared during fighting and struggle to address the need to protect noncombatants and prisoners during siege warfare. These sources also outline rules for the treatment of emissaries and messengers, along with foreign merchants, sometimes in great detail.

Parallels between the *siyar* works and modern conventions provide evidence for arguing that early Muslim scholars created a sophisticated system of international law that included ambassadors, rules of war, standards for international commerce, and even limited immunity for merchants and diplomats. These interpretations serve the twofold agenda of showing that Muslims preceded non-Muslim Europeans in establishing such norms for international relations and demonstrating that Islamic law is comprehensive, foreseeing and providing guidance for a world of modern nation-states.

As one of the earliest scholars of the laws of war, al-Awzaʿi plays a central role in these discussions. For those seeking Muslim origins of modern institutions, the earlier the better. It is doubtful that al-Awzaʿi and his Hanafi rivals had such grandiose ambitions. The *siyar* authors appear to have been concerned with more immediate, practical issues.

This modern reimagining of the *siyar*, the product of a confluence of the search for legal origins and the assertion of Muslim primacy, relies heavily on al-Awza'i and underscores his continuing importance as a legal scholar.

Contemporary events have led to a more unexpected resurgence in interest in al-Awza'i's opinions on specific legal matters as well. The advent of ISIS has brought with it a long list of horrors and destruction that are well known. ISIS has also had a peculiar effect on discourse about Islamic law. Its determination to reject long-standing norms in favor of its own vision of Islamic law, purportedly based on the practice of the early community, has led both ISIS and those refuting ISIS to rely heavily on early Islamic legal sources, occasionally including al-Awza'i. While ISIS' own legal discourse, such as it is, relies predominantly on *hadith* and Qur'an, often cited devoid of actual context, ISIS' often anonymous writers do occasionally invoke al-Awza'i. For instance, one ISIS publication notes al-Awza'i's fairly generic exhortation that people should marvel at creation and avoid hellfire. In a more pertinent example, al-Awza'i is praised for combining his scholarship and asceticism with life on the frontier defending the faith, in contrast to armchair scholars who did not match their teachings with practice. ISIS' opponents, however, have deployed al-Awza'i more specifically. In 2014, a diverse group of Muslim scholars penned an open letter to ISIS leader Abu Bakr al-Baghdadi refuting a long list of ISIS' practices and doctrines. The letter cites al-Awza'i's judgment that the *jizya* should be applied to Zoroastrians, in order to condemn ISIS' enslavement of Iraqi Yazidis. The letter eventually gained the endorsement of more than 125 prominent jurists. With 126,000 "likes," 24,000 Facebook shares, and a Twitter following, this is undoubtedly the most widely circulated citation of al-Awza'i ever. While tweets and retweets have become important markers in modern discourse, the fact that scholars on both sides of the fiercest ideological struggle in contemporary Islam choose to cite al-Awza'i at all is more important. It demonstrates that al-Awza'i's example and his specific legal solutions still command respect from a broad spectrum of modern scholars.

Al-Awzaʿi's legacy endures in the impact of his students, the continued application of his legal rulings, contemporary invocations of
his legal authority, and in modern reinterpretations of his work as a
precursor to modern international law. This is an impressive list of
accomplishments for the leader of a failed *madhhab* who supported a
defeated dynasty and died unceremoniously in the bath.

CONCLUSION

This examination of the life and thoughts of al-Awza'i underscores both the prospects and limitations of reconstructing the biographies of important early Islamic figures. Finding and evaluating sources for early Islamic history is, of course, a perennial problem. However, careful use of available materials can offer at least a general image of the scholars who shaped the emergence of Islamic law and theology, even those whose stories are not frequently told.

In the case of al-Awza'i, a complete understanding of the man and his ideas may be impossible to achieve. The evidence allows a credible reconstruction of his interactions with other early Muslim figures. However, his motivations, his opinions of those with whom he associated, and his purposes are harder to uncover. Such limitations are inherent to biographical research in general, even in cases where abundant sources are available. The gaps in information about al-Awza'i's scholarly itineraries, his finances, and his family are frustrating, but also not uncommon for the early Islamic period. There are lacunae in even the most copiously retold lives of famous early Muslim scholars.

Despite the impediments encountered, a reasonable reconstruction of al-Awza'i's views on important topics can be accomplished. His views on certain aspects of law and theology are portrayed in the sources with remarkable consistency, suggesting that his positions were both well known and agreed upon. In terms of theology, he was clearly a strong advocate for predestinarian views. Both his enmity toward the Qadarites and his approach to refuting them appear repeatedly and, again, consistently in later accounts. His views on other theological topics are less apparent. It is possible that the relative silence of the sources reflects a lack of interest in such questions on al-Awza'i's part or suggests that his views on some matters were unremarkable and did not merit much discussion. It is also possible that the Qadarite issue so dominated discussion that other topics were deemed less relevant. At the very least, al-Awza'i's position on the most pressing theological question of the day, as well as his rationale for his views, are well established.

Al-Awza'i's contribution to Islamic law is more difficult to assess. Later sources preserve his opinions on a wide variety of substantive legal issues. These are also remarkably consistent, suggesting that there was little disagreement about his views on a great number of specific legal topics. His solutions to sometimes tedious questions surrounding the laws of war are especially well preserved. In addition, his views on a wider array of legal questions can also be uncovered with relative ease, a reminder that al-Awza'i was more than just a frontier scholar. The search for a clearly articulated legal method behind his decisions is more frustrating. There are hints of a consistent approach to legal questions, but no comprehensive explanations of his theoretical methods. Instead, a mixture of past precedents, *hadith* references, and logical reasoning is evident. How al-Awza'i prioritized between these sources remains unclear. The fact that later scholars continued to cite his decisions and that they engaged in protracted arguments about his solutions to issues related to warfare underscores the respect that his views commanded and their longevity.

In addition to offering insights into the development of Islamic law and theology, al-Awza'i's biography also provides a lens through which to examine the social dynamics of the early Islamic scholarly world. Accounts of his interactions with other scholars illustrate the complexities of scholarly status and the underlying rationality of the networks he and others established and operated within. These networks were not regional, but personal. An understanding of professional rivalries, ideological rifts, and other interpersonal factors was crucial for scholars in al-Awza'i's era. Al-Awza'i's experience also underscores the complicated relationship between scholarly prestige and political power. He and his peers did not operate in a political vacuum. Their opinions on legal and other issues often had substantial political implications. While some scholars either insulated themselves from political circles or were uninvited there, al-Awza'i was a political animal. His close association with the Umayyads and his antipathy toward the Abbasids and their revolution are clear. The fact that he, unlike some of his colleagues, was never criticized for his embrace of the Umayyads and the fact that he survived a revolution he opposed and returned to public life, albeit in a different form, are as much a testament to his political acumen as to his reputation for piety and incorruptibility.

The state of the sources creates obvious difficulties for reconstructing al-Awza'i's life and thought. The fact that his *madhhab* was short-lived means that less was written about al-Awza'i by his acolytes and there was no systematic effort to compile and preserve his writings or to distill and explicate his methods. The stories of scholars with small followings are simply not told. Consequently, reconstructing al-Awza'i's influence has required an effort to glean material from sources written by followers of other schools for other purposes. While this process is tedious, it is also likely to offer a less distorted image of al-Awza'i than we have of other scholars. Scholars with large followings whose movements lasted for centuries attracted legendary accretions, hagiographic additions, and in some cases derogation from opponents. In many cases, it becomes difficult, perhaps even impossible, to sort truth from fiction in the biographies of famous figures in early Islam. In al-Awza'i's case, this is a less pressing concern. His biography was not preserved by fawning students or by defamatory opponents, with the exception perhaps of some material presented by Abu Yusuf. Instead, the fragments of al-Awza'i's activities and ideas are largely preserved by later scholars who respected his views on particular issues. It is quite possible that the biographies of less famous scholars such as al-Awza'i can be reconstructed with greater accuracy, though with less detail, than those of their more prominent peers.

This study of al-Awza'i is also a reminder of the importance of the Umayyad period, and Damascus specifically, for the intellectual development of Islam. Much of the scholarship on the development of Islamic law and theology errs by discounting Umayyad-era contributions and focusing too much attention on Iraq and the Abbasids.

Similarly, this study underscores the importance of moving beyond the focus on the surviving legal *madhhabs* and a few prominent theologians in reconstructing the early Islamic scholarly environment. A long list of less commonly known names contributed to the intellectual underpinning of the new faith in its formative period. Al-Awza'i is arguably the most significant and interesting of these largely forgotten scholars of the Umayyad period, but he was certainly not alone.

BIBLIOGRAPHY

ARABIC SOURCES

Abū Nuʿaym al-Iṣfahānī, Aḥmad b. ʿAbdallāh. *Ḥilyat al-awliyāʾ wa ṭabaqāt al-aṣfiyāʾ* (Beirut: Dār al-kutub al-ʿilmiyya, 1997).

Abū Yūsuf, Yaʿqūb b. Ibrāhīm. *al-Radd ʿalā siyar al-Awzāʿī* (Cairo, 1938).

Abū Zurʿa, ʿAbd al-Raḥmān. *Taʾrīkh Abī Zurʿa al-Dimashqī* (Damascus, 1981).

Al-Bukhārī, Muḥammad b. Ismāʿīl. *Jāmīʿ al-ṣaḥīḥ* (Beirut: Dār iḥyāʾ al-turāth al-ʿarabī, 1981).

Al-Dhahabī, Shams al-Dīn Muḥammad b. Aḥmad. *Siyar aʿlām al-nubalāʾ* (Beirut: Muʾassasat al-risāla, 1981).

al-Fazārī, Abū Isḥāq. *Kitāb al-siyar* (Beirut: Muʾassasat al-Risāla, 1987).

Ibn ʿAbd al-Barr. *Istidhkār al-jāmiʿ li-madhāhib fuqahāʾ al-amṣār* (Cairo, 1993).

Ibn Abī Ḥātim al-Rāzī. *Taqdimat al-maʿrifa li-kitāb al-jarḥ waʾl-taʿdīl* (Hyderabad, 1952).

Ibn ʿAsākir, ʿAlī b. al-Ḥasan. *Taʾrīkh madīnat Dimashq* (Beirut: Dār al-Fikr, 1995–2000).

Ibn Māja. *Sunan* (Cairo, 1952).

Ibn al-Nadīm. *al-Fihrist* (Beirut: Dār al-kitāb al-ʿilmiyya, 2002).

Muslim. *Ṣaḥīḥ* (Cairo, 1955).

Al-Shāfiʿī, Muḥammad b. Idrīs. *Kitāb al-Umm* (Bulaq, 1903).

Al-Ṭabarī, Abū Jaʿfar Muḥammad b. Jarīr. *Ikhtilāf al-fuqahāʾ: Konstantinopler Fragment des Kitāb iḫtilāf al-fuqahāʾ des Abū Ǧaʿfar Muḥammad ibn Ǧarīr aṭ-Ṭabarī*, ed. Joseph Schacht (Leiden: Brill, 1933).

Al-Ṭabarī, Abū Jaʿfar Muḥammad b. Jarīr, *Taʾrīkh al-rusul waʾl-mulūk* (Leiden: Brill, 1879–1901).

SOURCES IN WESTERN LANGUAGES

Bonner, Michael. *Aristocratic Violence and Holy War: Studies in the Jihad and the Arab-Byzantine Frontier* (New Haven: American Oriental Society, 1996).

Bouzenita, Anke. "Early Contributions to the Theory of Islamic Governance: 'Abd al-Raḥmān al-Awzā'ī." *Journal of Islamic Studies* 23 (2012): 137–164.

―――― "The Siyar: An Islamic Law of Nations?" *Asian Journal of Social Science* 35 (2007): 19–46.

―――― '*Abdarraḥmān al-Auzā'ī – ein Rechtsgelehrter des 2. Jahrhunderts d. H. und sein Beitrag zu den Siyar* (Berlin: Klaus Schwarz Verlag, 2001).

Chéhab, Maurice. *Mosaiques du Liban* (Paris: Librarie d'Amérique et d'Orient, 1957).

Conrad, Gerhard. *Die quḍāt Dimašq und der maḏhab al-Auzā'ī* (Beirut: Beiruter Texte und Studien, 1994).

Elad, Amikam. *The Rebellion of Muḥammad al-Nafs al-Zakiyya in 145/762: Ṭālibīs and Early 'Abbāsīs in Conflict* (Leiden: Brill, 2016).

Ess, Josef van. *Anfänge muslimischer Theologie* (Beirut: Beiruter Texte und Studien, 1977).

―――― *Theologie und Gesellschaft Im 2. Und 3. Jahrhundert Hidschra* (Berlin: Walter de Gruyter, 1991–97).

Idris, Hady-Roger. "Reflections on Malikism under the Umayyads of Spain." In *The Formation of al-Andalus: Part 2 Language, Religion, Culture and the Sciences*, edited by M. Fierro and J. Samsó, 85–101 (Aldershot: Ashgate, 1998).

Judd, Steven. "Al-Awzā'ī and Sufyān al-Thawrī: The Umayyad Madhhab?" In *The Islamic School of Law: Evolution, Devolution, and Progress*, edited by P. Bearman, F. Vogel, R. Peters, 10–25 (Cambridge: Harvard University Press, 2005).

―――― "Al-Awzā'ī and Umayyad Influence on Islamic Legal Development." In *The Umayyad World*, edited by A. Marsham (London: Routledge, 2019).

―――― "Competitive Hagiography in Biographies of Al-Awzā'ī and Sufyān al-Thawrī." *Journal of the American Oriental Society* 122 (2002): 25–37.

―――― "Ghaylān al-Dimashqī: The Isolation of a Heretic in Islamic Historiography." *International Journal of Middle East Studies* 31 (1999): 161–184.

―――― "Muslim Persecution of Heretics during the Marwānid Period (64–132/684–750)." *Al-Masāq* 23 (2011): 1–14.

―――― *Religious Scholars and the Umayyads: Piety-minded Supporters of the Marwānid Caliphate* (London: Routledge, 2014).

Mourad, Suleiman. *Early Islam between Myth and History: Al-Ḥasan al-Baṣrī (d. 110H/728CE) and the Formation of His Legacy in Classical Islamic Scholarship* (Leiden: Brill, 2006).

Open letter to Abu Bakr al-Baghdadi, 19 September 2014. (lettertobaghdadi. com)

Saha, Daniel. *John of Damascus on Islam* (Leiden: Brill, 1972).

Schacht, Joseph. *An Introduction to Islamic Law* (Oxford: Oxford University Press, 1964).

———— *Origins of Muhammadan Jurisprudence* (Oxford: Oxford University Press, 1950).

ath-Thaghri, Abul-Harith. "Contemplate the Creation." *Dabiq* 15 (2016): 8–9. (https://azelin.files.wordpress.com/2016/07/the-islamic-state-e2809c-dacc84biq-magazine-1522.pdf)

Tillier, Mathieu. *L'invention du cadi: la justice des musulmans, des juifs et des chrétiens aux premiers siècles de l'islam* (Paris: Sorbonne, 2017).

Tsafrir, Nurit. *The History of an Islamic School of Law: The Early Spread of Hanafism* (Cambridge: Harvard University Press, 2004).

Wellhausen, Julius. *Das arabische Reich und sein Sturz* (Berlin, 1902). Translated by M. G. Weir as *The Arab Kingdom and Its Fall* (London: Curzon, 1973).

Wensink, A. J. *The Muslim Creed: Its Genesis and Historical Development* (Cambridge: Cambridge University Press, 1932).

"The Wicked Scholars are Cursed." *Rumiyah* 1 (2016): 29–31. (https://azelin. files.wordpress.com/2016/09/rome-magazine-1.pdf)

INDEX